"Having spent many years treating depressed clients with behavioral activation, and being forced by circumstance to address post-traumatic stress disorder (PTSD) and PTSD symptoms as part of this work, I can state clearly that this book is necessary. Jakupcak, Wagner, and Martell combine a real empathic understanding of the lives, needs, and struggles of people with PTSD with expertise in behavioral activation to produce a useful, hands-on guide. At the core of many clinical problems, including PTSD, is avoidance, and this book offers the most practical and empathic analysis of avoidance that I have experienced. I expect the workbook will be helpful to both clients and their therapists."

—**Jonathan Kanter, PhD**, director of the Center for the Science of
Social Connection at the University of Washington

"People with mental health problems, including those with PTSD, tell us they want treatment choices that can be individualized, accessed easily, and which they can undertake at their own pace. Most importantly, they want treatments that work. In this book Jakupcak, Wagner, and Martell have delivered on all counts. They describe behavioral activation for PTSD, a scientifically proven treatment that people can use at their own pace, with easy-to-use instructions and plans. It is a book that will be warmly welcomed by those with PTSD, their friends and family, and by therapists alike. I heartily recommend it."

—**David A. Richards, PhD**, professor of mental health services research at the
University of Exeter in the UK; and chief investigator and author of the 'COBRA'
(Cost and Effectiveness of Behavioural Activation) clinical trial for *The Lancet*

"This is an excellent volume that clearly and practically outlines the rationale, principles, and core techniques of behavioral activation targeting PTSD. As noted in the introduction and documented throughout the extremely high-quality workbook, the authors are outstanding examples of clinician-investigators who have worked to apply the principles and techniques outlined in the volume in their own psychotherapy practices. The volume outlines how behavioral activation may be an excellent first step in the journey towards recovery from PTSD—an outstanding and articulate overview of behavioral activation from a group of pioneering clinician-investigators whose randomized trials have begun to establish the evidence base for behavioral activation as a mainstream PTSD treatment."

—**Doug Zatzick, MD**, professor in the department of psychiatry and behavioral sciences at the University of Washington School of Medicine

"Three of the field's most expert, skillful practitioners have created a much-needed, accessible resource for people experiencing PTSD. This step-by-step, evidence-based, clinically wise workbook will guide readers through practices that will help them rebuild their lives. I highly recommend this excellent, valuable, trustworthy guide to PTSD behavioral activation."

—**Lizabeth Roemer, PhD**, coauthor of *Worry Less, Live More*

"Matthew Jakupcak and colleagues have produced a genuinely meaningful and substantive contribution to the emotional well-being of trauma survivors. Behavioral activation effectively addresses mood difficulties while simultaneously targeting PTSD avoidance symptoms that maintain post-traumatic stress. This approach is meticulously researched and evidence-based. Importantly, it renders effective treatment readily accessible to trauma survivors who would otherwise not be able to access mental health support. This workbook—whether utilized as a self-help resource or in conjunction with a therapist—will appreciably benefit clients in ways that existing resources do not. I will be relying on it regularly in my own clinical practice."

—**Matt J. Gray, PhD**, professor of psychology at the University of Wyoming

"The authors provide a highly practical and easy-to-read workbook on how behavioral activation can be used to help the millions of people suffering from PTSD. The authors use vivid examples and easy-to-use worksheets to help the reader quickly learn how to apply this evidence-based approach. While there are other effective therapies for PTSD, behavioral activation has been shown to have particularly high acceptance among diverse patient populations. Combined with its effectiveness for treating depression, which is commonly comorbid with PTSD, behavioral activation should be considered as a core component of PTSD treatment. Clinicians and trainees alike will find this text to be an incredibly valuable tool for their practice."

—**Jesse Fann, MD, MPH**, professor of psychiatry and behavioral sciences, and adjunct professor of rehabilitation medicine and epidemiology at the University of Washington; and medical director of psychiatry and psychology at Seattle Cancer Care Alliance

"*The PTSD Behavioral Activation Workbook* is a scientifically supported, user-friendly guide that provides an indispensable toolkit for rebuilding your life from PTSD. This long-awaited alternative to trauma-focused treatments for PTSD offers present-centered strategies to help you start living a more fulfilling, value-driven life while promoting recovery from PTSD. I have found behavioral activation for PTSD to be both well received and effective in my own clinical practice and research."

—**Jessica Cook, PhD**, associate professor at the University of Wisconsin School of Medicine and Public Health

THE PTSD
Behavioral
Activation
WORKBOOK

ACTIVITIES *to* HELP YOU
REBUILD YOUR LIFE *from*
POST-TRAUMATIC STRESS DISORDER

MATTHEW JAKUPCAK, PhD
AMY WAGNER, PhD
CHRISTOPHER R. MARTELL, PhD, ABPP

New Harbinger Publications, Inc.

Publisher's Note

NEW HARBINGER PUBLICATIONS is a registered trademark of New Harbinger Publications, Inc.

Distributed in Canada by Raincoast Books

Copyright © 2019 by Matthew Jakupcak, Amy Wagner, & Christopher Martell
New Harbinger Publications, Inc.
5674 Shattuck Avenue
Oakland, CA 94609
www.newharbinger.com

Cover design by Amy Shoup

Acquired by Jennye Garibaldi

Edited by Rona Bernstein

Library of Congress Cataloging-in-Publication Data on file

Printed in the United States of America

23   22   21

10   9   8   7   6   5   4   3   2

Contents

Foreword

Posttraumatic stress disorder (PTSD) is a serious condition that can have a negative impact on many domains of a person's life. Fortunately, we are at a place in time where the symptoms of PTSD can be effectively treated through psychological interventions. Although PTSD has been recognized throughout history by different names (e.g., shell shock, combat fatigue), PTSD as we know it today is a relatively young condition, first appearing as an official diagnosis in 1980. Since that time, there has been an exponential growth in research on the treatment of PTSD. Through this research, "gold standard" psychological treatments for PTSD have been identified, particularly prolonged exposure and cognitive processing therapy. There is no question that these treatments have helped many people with PTSD. However, they are effective only to the extent that people can access them or are at a place where they can benefit from them. Thus, a major challenge is identifying other effective treatment options for people with PTSD. Behavioral activation for PTSD represents one such option.

Although behavioral activation would not be considered a new treatment, this workbook does have something new to offer. The information and skills presented in this book are innovative and represent current thought on best practices for the treatment of mental health conditions. There has recently been a push in the field for the development of transdiagnostic treatments—that is, psychological treatments that can be broadly applied to people with different mental health conditions (Craske 2012). Behavioral activation fits this mold. Behavioral activation was originally conceptualized to treat the symptoms of depression. However, recent research (some of which was conducted by the authors of this workbook) shows that behavioral activation can also be beneficial for people with PTSD (Jakupcak et al. 2010; Wagner et al. 2007) and other mental health conditions (Dimidjian et al. 2011). This is not entirely surprising because, at its core, behavioral activation aims to reduce the avoidance behavior that is central to the maintenance of PTSD and other mental health problems that commonly co-occur with PTSD. The skills presented in this workbook directly target this avoidance by helping you identify and increase valued and rewarding activities. In doing so, you can develop a sense of mastery, as well as an understanding that the symptoms of PTSD do not have to be a barrier to building and living the life you want to live.

This workbook is also innovative in its incorporation of mindfulness into behavioral activation. Mindfulness holds promise as an evidence-based psychological intervention (Goldberg et al. 2018), and studies have found that it can benefit people with PTSD in particular (Boyd, Lanius, and McKinnon 2018). Symptoms of PTSD (e.g., intrusive thoughts) can pull people out of the present moment, preventing them from experiencing the naturally rewarding consequences of engaging in valued action. The authors have skillfully applied this research in their presentation of mindfulness skills. Specifically, they show how mindfulness can facilitate and increase the benefits of behavioral activation, further reducing PTSD's grip on your life.

This evidence-based workbook is a valuable resource and a welcome addition to the available options for people looking for ways to manage the symptoms of PTSD. Addressing the symptoms of PTSD can feel like a daunting task; however, this workbook can serve as an effective and compassionate guide through your recovery from PTSD. As you progress through this workbook, you will notice that the skills are presented in a clear, uncomplicated, and validating manner. Regardless of where you are in your recovery from PTSD, this workbook will help you develop an individualized and comprehensive plan for coping with the symptoms of PTSD. It is clear that Drs. Jakupcak, Wagner, and Martell are skilled clinicians and researchers who are sensitive to the needs of their patients. Their workbook represents the culmination of years of research on the best treatment approaches for PTSD and other mental health conditions. As such, there is no doubt this workbook will be of benefit to people working to build and live a meaningful life unobstructed by PTSD.

—Matthew T. Tull, Ph.D.
Professor, Department of Psychology,
University of Toledo, Ohio

Introduction

Welcome to *The PTSD Behavioral Activation Workbook*! We appreciate your effort to cope with the trauma you have experienced and are hopeful this can be a useful part of your recovery. We have designed this workbook for individuals with posttraumatic stress disorder (PTSD) symptoms to use either individually to self-guide their recovery or within the context of treatment with a health care provider (e.g., psychologist, counselor, social worker, nurse, or other type of medical provider). Whichever way you choose to use it, we encourage you to adopt a pace that makes sense to you. It might be helpful to reread certain chapters and practice exercises repeatedly until you feel comfortable with each set of behavioral activation skills. We also encourage you to share the workbook with important people in your life, such as a spouse or close friend(s), so that they can learn more about PTSD and your recovery goals.

Before we begin, we'd like to share a bit about ourselves and how we came to develop and use behavioral activation in our work with individuals who have experienced traumatic life events. We are clinical psychologists with a wide range of therapy and research experiences (collectively, over seventy-five years' worth!). We've worked in universities, veterans' medical centers, and private practices; with adults of all ages; with different ethnic, racial, and cultural groups (including the military); and with members of the LGBTQ community. Christopher has expertise in the treatment of depression and was one of the original developers of behavioral activation for depression (considered one of the most effective treatments for depression). Two of us, Matthew and Amy, have devoted our careers to the treatment of PTSD and have worked with individuals with a wide range of traumatic experiences. Over the years and through our breadth of experiences, we have come to appreciate that, although the *types* of PTSD symptoms are similar across individuals, people experience traumatic symptoms in unique ways that differently impact their daily lives. Further, we recognize that there are many different paths toward recovery from PTSD. While some people benefit from talking through their experiences (as in trauma-processing therapies), others prefer a more present-focused, action-oriented approach.

We appreciate the emphasis in behavioral activation on tailoring the treatment to your unique values and goals. As clinicians, we follow some core principles about human behavior and rely on our psychological understanding of PTSD, depression, anxiety, and other problems, but we need to understand each person's unique experience before embarking on the treatment. That is exciting to us because people are more than a diagnosis; *you* are more than a diagnosis or a problem. Behavioral activation is structured to help you connect with important people, places, and activities that may have become less prominent in your life since your traumatic experience. We decided to write this workbook as a tool to help you on the way.

You are likely reading this workbook because you (or someone close to you) is experiencing symptoms of PTSD. This might be your first attempt to address your PTSD symptoms, or you may have already tried different treatments for PTSD but found that you are still struggling in your life because of your traumatic stress symptoms. It is likely that your PTSD symptoms are getting in the way of living the type of life you want to live.

As we outline in the next chapters, PTSD probably causes you to avoid certain activities, getting in the way of personal goals or meaningful relationships that would enrich your life. PTSD also may cause you to feel numb or detached in your daily life, so you might find yourself "going through the motions" but not enjoying activities that would otherwise help you experience satisfaction and happiness.

The primary aims of behavioral activation for PTSD are to help you identify the ways that avoidance, numbing, and detachment are interfering with your quality of life and to develop some alternative ways that you can reengage in the experiences that you value and that will help you recover from PTSD. We hope the information and strategies we outline in this workbook will be helpful to you and assist you in getting your life back on track. Several of the exercises as well as some other materials are available on the website for this book, http://www.newharbinger.com/43072; see the very back of this book for more details. You can download and print copies of these exercises and materials to use again at a later date.

Although we have designed this workbook as a self-help resource to promote your recovery from PTSD, we believe that having outside support and encouragement from a trusted loved one or a mental health provider will help you use the behavioral activation strategies to change your life. We encourage you to consider which people in your life you can reach out to for support as you use this workbook, share with them the information you learn from the workbook and identify your goals for recovery so that they can support your efforts.

Before we begin to describe more about behavioral activation, we want to first make sure you have a good understanding of PTSD. Although you may have been living with these symptoms for a long time, it can be helpful to learn about what medical and mental health professionals look for when they are trying to identify PTSD.

What Is PTSD?

PTSD is a mental health diagnosis that applies to the difficulties some people experience following exposure to a traumatic event. PTSD is one of the few mental health conditions that specifically cites an outside event as the cause for the disorder. So, before describing the symptoms of PTSD, we want to first outline what constitutes a traumatic event.

Many types of experiences might cause you to feel a great deal of stress, but not all stressful events are considered traumatic events. For example, if you have gone through a difficult divorce or financial bankruptcy, you likely experienced high levels of stress for extended periods of time. However, these aren't the types of events that typically represent psychological trauma. Rather, traumatic events are those that immediately threaten a person's life or physical well-being. Traumatic events might be directly experienced (e.g., being involved in a serious motor vehicle accident) or witnessed (seeing others hurt by a serious motor vehicle accident). Other types of traumatic events experienced or witnessed include natural disasters, interpersonal assault (e.g., sexual or physical abuse or assault), and military combat.

Traumatic events often cause major disruptions in peoples' lives and typically change how people view themselves or the world in significant ways. In general, the more "personal" the type of traumatic event, the more likely it is to lead to PTSD. For example, if you have experienced intentional violence from another person, you may be more likely to develop PTSD than you would be if you were exposed to an earthquake (which might feel less personal). This may be because a natural disaster is clearly a random event, whereas being intentionally hurt by another human being can negatively impact your general trust of other human beings or cause you to doubt your ability to identify "safe" relationships.

Further, if you experience multiple traumatic events across your lifetime, you may be more likely to develop PTSD than you might if you experienced a single traumatic event. That said, we have found that most of our clients tend to downplay their own traumatic history, perhaps feeling as though they need to minimize their traumas when they compare them to "what other people have experienced." If you have been exposed to trauma and you have developed symptoms of PTSD, you deserve help recovering from the symptoms and rebuilding a meaningful life.

It is also important to keep in mind that many people are exposed to potentially traumatic events but do *not* go on to develop a full spectrum of PTSD symptoms. For example, if you have experienced a "fender bender" car accident, you may feel compelled to check the rearview mirror at every stop sign and drive with an increased vigilance toward other vehicles. You may also think about the accident frequently for several weeks or even have dreams about the car accident. However, you might also find that this is transitory and that over several weeks, the hypervigilance and intrusive thoughts of the accident subside. Even if you experience a full range of PTSD symptoms, you might find that after several weeks, you are mostly feeling back to your normal self. When symptoms last less than one month, we refer to this as an *acute stress reaction*. However, when posttraumatic stress symptoms persist more than a few weeks and begin to negatively impact a person's ability to function in work and personal life domains, we use the term *posttraumatic stress disorder*, or PTSD.

In the exercise below, we provide you details about each of the PTSD symptoms and what combination of symptoms constitutes a formal PTSD diagnosis to help you determine whether you might meet some or all the criteria.

Self-Assessment Exercise

Below is the list of PTSD symptoms defined by the fifth edition of the *Diagnostic and Statistical Manual of Mental Disorders* (*DSM*-5; American Psychiatric Association [APA] 2013), used by medical and mental health providers. Place a check mark next to those symptoms that you have experienced in the past month:

Criterion A. Exposure to death, threatened death, serious injury (or threat of serious injury), or actual or threatened sexual violence. This can involve

- ☐ direct exposure (experiencing the event oneself), witnessing the event, learning of a loved one/family member's exposure to trauma, or

- ☐ indirect but repeated exposure to trauma details experienced by others during the course of professional duties (e.g., police, firefighters, or paramedics who routinely are exposed to others' traumatic experiences).

Criterion B. The traumatic event is reexperienced in *at least one* of the following ways:

- ☐ Intrusive thoughts or memories of the trauma

- ☐ Nightmares/dreams of the trauma

- ☐ "Flashbacks" involving sights, sounds, smells, or other sensory experiences that appear vividly

- ☐ Emotional distress in response to reminders of the trauma

- ☐ Physical reactions (e.g., racing heart rate, sweating, shaking) in response to reminders of the trauma

Criterion C. *At least one* type of avoidance pattern evidenced by:

- ☐ Avoidance of trauma-related thoughts or emotions
- ☐ Avoidance of external reminders (places, people, images) of the trauma

Criterion D. *At least two* changes in thoughts or emotions following trauma, as evidenced by:

- ☐ Difficulty remembering key elements of the traumatic event
- ☐ Overly negative views of oneself or the world
- ☐ Distortions in blame toward oneself or others related to the trauma
- ☐ Negative emotions (e.g., shame, guilt, anxiety, anger)
- ☐ Decreased interest in or enjoyment of activities
- ☐ Social isolation or emotional detachment from others
- ☐ Difficulties experiencing positive emotions (e.g., love or happiness)

Criterion E. *Two or more* types of trauma-related physical arousal or emotional reactivity demonstrated by:

- ☐ Persistent irritability or aggression
- ☐ Risky or self-destructive behaviors
- ☐ Extreme vigilance to one's surroundings or safety
- ☐ Strong startle reactions (e.g., jumping in response to noises or movement)
- ☐ Difficulty concentrating
- ☐ Difficulty sleeping

You may have been already diagnosed with PTSD by a medical or mental health professional and have turned to this workbook as an additional tool for helping you to cope and overcome the symptoms that trouble you. Or perhaps you have suspected that you have PTSD but have not received a formal diagnosis. If you checked at least one reexperiencing symptom (Cluster B), one avoidance symptom (Cluster C), two alterations in thoughts or emotions (Cluster D), and two arousal or emotional reactivity symptoms (Cluster E), and if these symptoms cause disruptions in one or more important areas of your life, you may likely meet criteria for PTSD. Keep in mind that PTSD symptoms can range in severity from mild to severe. Even if your symptoms are mild or you do not meet all the criteria for PTSD, this workbook could still be of use to you.

The above self-assessment exercise can help you begin to explore whether you might have PTSD. However, no self-assessment is ever a good replacement for speaking to a licensed mental health or medical professional for diagnosis and treatment. We are providing this assessment for you to use as a guide only. Just as we've said that experiencing some of these symptoms for a brief period following a traumatic event is common, we also want to point out that it is common for people to read lists of symptoms and conclude that they have the condition when they may not. If you think you may have PTSD and have never consulted a mental health or medical professional, we encourage you to do so.

Why Do Some People Develop PTSD After a Traumatic Event and Others Don't?

We have already mentioned that many people experience traumatic events but do not go on to develop PTSD, whereas others develop PTSD and may suffer from these symptoms for many years without relief. If your self-assessment (above) suggests that you may have PTSD, you may be wondering what made you vulnerable to the development of PTSD.

A number of factors are thought to contribute to the onset of PTSD, including biological factors (that is, a biological predisposition that may be reflected in family histories of depression, anxiety, or other mental illnesses), situational factors (for example, having low emotional support or access to physical safety following trauma exposure), and the type and degree of trauma exposure (some traumas, such as sexual assault or combat exposure are more likely to cause PTSD than other traumas, such as motor vehicle accidents or natural disasters, and a history of multiple traumatic events is more likely to lead to PTSD than a single event).

Although all human beings are vulnerable to developing PTSD, we know that some people who experience traumatic events are able to react, readjust, and resume their lives without developing chronic PTSD. Why is it that some people do *not* develop PTSD or recover more quickly than others? It appears that a key part of this resilience from trauma and recovery from PTSD is the degree to which a person is able to resume regular routines, stay connected to family and friends, and continue to pursue personal goals and meaningful activities.

In many ways, this natural resilience and recovery process is exactly what we try and promote in behavioral activation for PTSD. When you continue (or resume) your regular activities after a traumatic event, you are likely exposing yourself to some triggers that prompt you to recall the memories of the traumatic event. However, if you find ways to "push through" the triggered responses so that you can maintain important routines, you will probably learn to adjust to the triggers over time, lessening the associations between people and places you encounter and the memory of your traumatic event(s).

Also, if you can maintain or reestablish close personal relationships, these relationships will most likely help you by giving you encouragement and emotional support. You might even choose to share some details of your traumatic events with those closest to you, thus helping you process what you have gone through. And if you continue to work toward your personal goals in life, you may be better able to overcome feelings of depression or hopelessness, build positive self-esteem, and reestablish confidence in your abilities to navigate challenges in the world.

The natural recovery process is different from simply "going through the motions" of daily life while suppressing or hiding PTSD symptoms. Unlike avoidance or suppression efforts used to "hide" PTSD, the recovery process recognizes the impact of the trauma and finds constructive ways to navigate PTSD symptoms until they lessen over time through meaningful engagement in life. It is a lot like the difference between letting a car coast in neutral gear and putting it into drive; they might look the same to an outside observer, but putting your life in gear toward recovery gives you more control and better abilities to navigate the road toward reclaiming your life from PTSD. If you have become "stuck" in PTSD symptoms, try not to become discouraged. We have seen many people restart the recovery process after decades of living with PTSD. Indeed, we developed behavioral activation strategies for PTSD in order to help you "reset" your life toward a path of recovery from PTSD.

As we will discuss later in the workbook, the strategies that we outline here are based on our research studies as well as our collective clinical experience using behavioral activation to help people overcome PTSD and depression. We will describe two "case examples" below that we follow throughout the workbook so that you can see how our clients have used behavioral activation to promote their recovery from PTSD. These case examples are composites, or blended depictions of actual clients we have worked with, mixed and disguised enough to protect the individuals' privacy. The details include real experiences we've addressed using behavioral activation to assist with recovery from PTSD.

We are aware that people with PTSD often become "triggered" when reading about trauma (or even hearing descriptions of the symptoms of PTSD). For this reason, we have intentionally limited the details of the traumatic events themselves, instead focusing on the symptoms of PTSD and how they caused disruptions in the lives of the people with whom we have worked. Nonetheless, be mindful of the potential to get triggered when reading this workbook. We encourage you to pace yourself so that you can pay attention to each chapter, take breaks if necessary, and plan pleasant or relaxing activities to help calm yourself should you become triggered.

Case Examples

In our two case examples, we include details of the individuals' personal qualities, trauma histories, and goals. Our intent is to help you see the relevance of behavioral activation to actual people—and to you in particular. However, we realize that everyone's experience is unique and that you may or may not be able to relate to these examples. Also, reading details of others' trauma can be difficult. If you prefer, you can skip the case examples described below—this won't affect what you get out of the workbook! (Although these cases are referred to throughout the workbook, the specific traumatic experiences will not be further mentioned.)

Karl

Karl came to therapy because he was struggling after his second combat deployment to Iraq. Karl served as a marine infantryman and had participated in the initial US invasion of Iraq in 2003. He found that the invasion was stressful, and he witnessed many people hurt and killed during this tour; however, he felt good about his service and was looking forward to another deployment when he was deployed again to Iraq a year later. It was during this second deployment that Karl participated in an intense battle in the area of Fallujah. During this battle, Karl experienced multiple and extended firefights. It was also during this battle that one of Karl's closest friends was killed by enemy fire, an event that Karl witnessed personally. Since that time, Karl began experiencing intense feelings of anger and guilt (he felt that he should have been killed instead of his close friend because his friend had a wife and family and Karl was single and had no children at the time). While still in Iraq, Karl began to emotionally distance himself from the other marines in his unit. Both Karl and his friend who had been killed were African-American, and Karl noticed that he felt more reactive to racial comments made toward Iraqis by other marines.

After he returned from his second deployment but before he separated from active duty military service, Karl began to have nightmares of some of the firefights he experienced during the battle. He also noticed that he was more easily startled ("jumpy") and felt keyed up, especially later in the evening when he was trying to get ready for bed. He began to drink large amounts of alcohol before going to bed to "pass out" and because he noticed that drinking tended to lessen his recall of the nightmares. When he complained of sleep difficulties to his unit's corpsman, he was referred to a mental health provider on base, who diagnosed him with PTSD. This caused Karl to feel shame, as he had previously prided himself on being "mentally tough," and he worried what other marines in his unit would think of him now that he had been diagnosed with PTSD. He also began to feel as though the military had "used" him without concern for his ultimate well-being ("they used me up and threw me away"), a sharp contrast to how he viewed his military service when he first enlisted.

Karl continued to struggle with PTSD symptoms, although he did his best to hide his symptoms from others. His military doctors prescribed him sleep medications, but he seldom took them because he feared becoming "dependent on pills." He was also referred to psychotherapy to address his PTSD, but he didn't find it helpful, and instead found that the therapist's efforts to get him to talk about the firefights in Fallujah and the death of his friend only made him feel angrier and more hopeless ("I felt worse after the sessions than I did before I started"). Eventually, Karl was medically discharged from the Marine Corps with a diagnosis of PTSD. He had previously hoped to stay in the military for most of his career, but when he was discharged, Karl felt that the Marine Corps had "broken" him, and he felt a great deal of resentment and regret regarding his military service.

After several years of struggling following his military separation, Karl finally decided to give therapy "another chance," in part because he had met a woman and become engaged to be married. He had worked at several jobs but often quit or was fired due to issues related to poor concentration, irritability, or irregular attendance. Karl wasn't sure if he could get his life back on track, but he was convinced that his PTSD symptoms "weren't going anywhere" unless he took a chance. That said, Karl was deeply skeptical of psychotherapy and reluctant to revisit the memories of his military service.

Annie

Annie is a divorced woman in her early thirties who came to therapy because she was having increasing difficulties at work, in her relationships, and parenting her two school-aged daughters. She described having high anxiety whenever she left her home and had particular difficulty in situations where people might be physically close (standing behind her at work, in elevators, in line at grocery stores, and in her gym). She said she felt "unsafe" in these situations and feared being attacked (if her daughters were with her, she feared for their safety as well). Often when she had high anxiety, she also had distressing memories of two sexual assaults she had experienced (one when she was in college by a stranger at a party and one last year on a first date). She was having increasing nightmares several times a week as well as difficulty falling and staying asleep. As a result,

Annie was becoming more and more withdrawn and isolated. She often called in sick to work or left early, and her work performance was suffering. She is a social worker at a medical center and previously received awards for her service and contributions, but at the time she entered therapy was concerned she would be fired or would need to quit. She was becoming overly protective of her daughters and did not feel comfortable with their participating in activities when she was not present (like parties or sleepovers with friends). Annie had stopped going to the gym and had not been socializing with her friends. She felt depressed and down on herself for, as she put it, "letting my life fall apart."

Annie's main goal was to be "a good mom" to her two daughters. She wanted to feel comfortable letting them do activities on their own and wanted them to feel safe and confident in the world ("I don't want to pass this on to them"). She also expressed a desire to "get my life back" but felt paralyzed by her anxiety and depression.

We have introduced you to Karl and Annie to help you see how PTSD can impact the lives of people exposed to traumatic events. However, keep in mind that no two people experience trauma in the same way, so you are likely to find differences as well as commonalities when reading their stories.

How Is Behavioral Activation Different from Other PTSD Therapies?

You may have already sought out psychotherapy for PTSD or researched other treatment approaches for PTSD. Behavioral activation shares many features with other approaches to treating trauma. However, it can be useful for you to understand how this approach differs from other psychotherapies for PTSD. Here's a brief description of some of the other evidence-based treatments (i.e., therapies that have been demonstrated to be useful in research studies) used to address PTSD.

The most well-established psychotherapies for PTSD are what we call "trauma-focused" therapies. Trauma-focused psychotherapies emphasize cognitive and emotional processing, or "talking through" the traumatic events and the thoughts and emotions linked to those traumatic events. These therapy approaches are based on the premise that in order to reclaim your life, you need to first confront the trauma memories (or at least the ways that the trauma changed the way you view yourself or the world).

Common and effective trauma-focused therapies include prolonged exposure (PE), cognitive processing therapy (CPT), and eye-movement desensitization and reprocessing (EMDR).

We want to emphasize that these therapies have been tested in many research studies and found to help many people with PTSD. They are typically delivered by therapists who have undergone extensive training in these approaches. So in no way do we wish to convey that they don't work. Just the opposite—we know that they are helpful for many people suffering from PTSD, and if you have not tried these approaches, we encourage you to consider these options.

However, in our experience, many people have difficulty accessing these therapies due to lack of availability in their area; if you live in a rural area, there might not be any therapists who have been trained in PE, CPT, or EMDR. Time commitment may also be a barrier for many individuals with PTSD. For example, PE therapy involves at least nine or ten sessions, each lasting typically ninety minutes or more. There is also the issue of cost; paying for therapy without insurance can be expensive, often ranging from $75 to $200 per visit (even simply the cost of insurance copays can add up to several hundred dollars over the course of treatment).

Yet an even more common barrier to people accessing these trauma-focused therapies is the expectation that clients share details of their trauma with their therapist early in treatment (typically in the first two or three visits). It can be easy for therapists, especially those who work with PTSD frequently, to lose an appreciation for how hard it might be to open up to a virtual stranger and share details of some of the worst moments of their lives. Indeed, several research studies have found that 20 to 50% of people who begin trauma-focused therapies drop out before completing them (Imel et al. 2013; Schottenbauer et al. 2008). In many ways, this shouldn't be surprising. Remember, avoidance is a core feature of PTSD and is considered to be a primary reason PTSD persists over time. So, the avoidance symptoms of PTSD literally represent barriers to people accessing therapies that might help them recover.

These are exactly the reasons we developed behavioral activation to help people with PTSD jump-start their recovery. Behavioral activation represents an alternative therapy that might be more appealing or accessible to those who would not otherwise engage in trauma-focused psychotherapies because of avoidance. It is not that we don't see the value of processing traumatic events. It is more simply that talking about the details of traumatic memories is perhaps too high of a bar for many people when they first seek help for PTSD. We have also been struck by the fact that several large, well-designed research studies have recently found that, comparing trauma-focused therapies to present-centered, problem-solving type therapies, the clinical outcomes are generally the same over the period of six to twelve months after starting treatment (e.g., Hoge and Chard 2018). So as the old saying goes, "There are many roads that lead to Rome." We believe that behavioral activation represents an alternative path to people for whom processing their traumatic memories is either too difficult at present or not what they want, or when trauma-focused therapy is not practically available.

How Do I Know If Behavioral Activation for PTSD Is the Right Approach for Me?

Overall, behavioral activation strategies are helpful when applied to most personal challenges in life. The core components of behavioral activation include individualized goal setting, planned and incremental steps toward personal goals, and active problem-solving strategies to work around challenges or barriers. All these skills are commonly used in the fields of education, business, and personal growth to help people make changes in their lives. As we said above, behavioral activation is one of the most effective treatments for depression. Further, Matthew, Amy, and other researchers have conducted numerous studies on behavioral activation for PTSD and have shown it can significantly reduce PTSD symptoms. For all these reasons, we believe behavioral activation skills are useful for anyone who is experiencing trauma reactions.

As we mentioned earlier, trauma-focused therapies are also highly effective in reducing PTSD and improving a person's quality of life. So if you feel ready to talk about your traumatic experiences with a therapist experienced in treating PTSD, you might consider these other types of therapy. If trauma-focused therapies sound as though they might be helpful to you, you still might use behavioral activation strategies to promote your recovery, either before, during, or after you complete an alternative therapy. Behavioral activation is in no way contradictory to these other approaches.

However, if you are newer to seeking mental health services or are hesitant to revisit your trauma memories as part of therapy, behavioral activation for PTSD might be a good first step in your recovery. Behavioral activation might also be a good choice if you tend to prefer action-based solutions versus inward, reflective, or emotional processing ways of coping. Finally, because behavioral activation is an intuitive, relatively simple approach to promoting recovery from PTSD, it may lend itself better to self-guided recovery efforts since it doesn't require any special training or deep knowledge of psychological theory.

How Do I Prepare for Behavioral Activation?

Whenever you begin a new approach to address a longstanding problem, it can help to prepare by reviewing what you have tried in the past and evaluating your readiness to try something new. We encourage you to take a few minutes to complete this brief preparation exercise to help you get ready to take action to recover from PTSD:

Preparing for Behavioral Activation

1. What types of therapies (if any) have I already tried to address my trauma/PTSD?

    _____

    _____

    _____

2. If you have tried other therapy approaches for addressing your PTSD, what worked well and what didn't work well?

    Things that worked well:

    _____

    _____

    _____

    Things that didn't work well:

    _____

    _____

    _____

3. Can I already identify some avoidance patterns associated with my PTSD? Briefly describe them, along with the "costs" associated with avoidance:

    Avoidance Pattern   Cost of Avoidance

    _____

    _____

    _____

    _____

    _____

    _____

_____

_____

_____

4.   How ready am I to try to make some changes in my daily routines?

Not ready   Somewhat ready   Very ready

1--------2--------3--------4--------5--------6--------7------8-------9--------10

Keep in mind, even if you don't feel as ready as you would like to be with regard to making changes in your daily routines, you are reading this workbook, which indicates you are at least thinking about ways you can recover from PTSD!

5.   What are some things that might help motivate me to make changes in my life? (for example, focusing on the benefits to your health or relationships that might come with change):

_____

_____

_____

Congratulations, you have now taken an important behavioral activation step by starting this workbook! Behavioral activation is about building momentum by taking manageable steps to reclaim your life. We invite you to continue. In chapter 1, we provide a more detailed orientation to behavioral activation and outline how you can use these strategies to start on your path toward recovery from PTSD.

CHAPTER 1

Orientation to Behavioral Activation for PTSD

As you embark on your journey toward recovery, we want to tell you about the learning principles on which behavioral activation is based, more about what behavioral activation is, and how this approach works. We will revisit the case examples of Karl and Annie to illustrate how to identify the initial focus and goals of behavioral activation. Finally, we will ask you to start considering your patterns of avoidance and thinking about how this approach can apply to you.

What Is Behavioral Activation Based On?

First, let's look at the behavioral (learning) principles that guide behavioral activation.

PTSD as a Learned Response

Psychological models of trauma hold that PTSD develops through *learned conditioning*, meaning that a traumatic event becomes *associated*, or paired in your memory, with things in the environment in which the trauma occurred. Sights, sounds, and smells that are present during exposure to traumatic events often become "triggers" for later PTSD reactions because of this conditioning process. For example, many of the Vietnam War era veterans with whom we have worked find that wet, overgrown foliage can serve as a PTSD trigger, reminding them of their combat experiences in jungle terrain. In contrast, many of the Iraq War era veterans report that dry, sandy, and hot climates cue their trauma reactions. So the setting in which the trauma occurs can often serve as a trigger for traumatic memories and reactions. Over time, this learned conditioning generalizes to similar situations.

So when you were exposed to your traumatic event(s), your brain associated the details of the situation and circumstances in which you were traumatized with the traumatic event itself, as well as with your emotional reactions (e.g., anxiety or fear) during the event. These are now conditioned reminders of the original event. When you later come across these conditioned reminders in *new environments*, you might be reminded of the original traumatic event and experience anxiety or fear, causing the new situation to become "contaminated" by the trauma memory and the difficult emotions that accompany it. In this way, PTSD memories cause triggered responses to migrate from the original setting of the trauma event to new settings or situations.

For example, if you experienced trauma within the context of a personal relationship, you may have learned that allowing yourself to become emotionally close to others is dangerous. Thus, after the traumatic exposure, you might find that developing new relationships is difficult because, when you begin to get close with someone new, your brain remembers the trauma and sends out anxiety and fear signals. Even if the new people you meet intend you no harm, the memory of trauma within one specific relationship becomes generalized to all relationships. And because of this, you may begin to avoid situations where you might come into contact with people who might want to get to know you. At first this may seem to work well for you, but over time, there is likely a higher price paid for your avoidance patterns. So it is important to understand why PTSD-related avoidance tends to persist (and even grow) over time.

Reinforcement

Things that tend to "work" for us in our lives do so because of the principle of reinforcement. *Reinforcement* refers to anything that follows a specific behavior that increases the chance that the behavior will occur again. When something is *added* after a behavior and makes it occur more often (like praise, money, a pleasant sensation or emotion), we call this *positive* reinforcement. Kindergarten teachers nationwide use positive reinforcement (in the forms of stickers and praise) to reinforce children learning how to pay attention in class and master the fundamentals of reading. When something unpleasant is *removed* by a behavior, this also makes the behavior that removed the unpleasantness more likely. For example, taking an aspirin to alleviate a headache helps us learn to use this medicine to remove pain, increasingly the likelihood that we will reach for aspirin for relief the next time we have headache pain; this is called *negative* reinforcement.

When traumatic life events happen, it is natural to withdraw or avoid, as many daily situations (people, places, or activities) might trigger memories of the trauma and bring up anxiety, stress, or fear. So avoidance is, naturally, negatively reinforced by the removal (or at least the decrease) of difficult emotions associated with traumatic memories. However, in the long run, avoidance makes it difficult to have opportunities for positive reinforcement—if you are engaged in avoidance, you are less likely to do things that could give you meaning or pleasure. Without a sense of meaning or the experience of pleasure, it becomes harder to be motivated to set goals or take steps to improve your life. Also, if you withdraw from situations and experiences that are *associated* reminders of your trauma (but not themselves dangerous), you miss out on opportunities to relearn that they are actually not dangerous (and therefore work through your trauma). This is exactly the type of learning pattern that behavioral activation targets and tries to reverse.

Behavioral activation targets common forms of PTSD-related avoidance, including social isolation (avoidance of interactions with others), emotional detachment (avoidance of experiencing or sharing emotions), and avoidance of reminders of traumatic memories (avoidance of situations or thoughts that prompt trauma memories). Behavioral activation can also be used to address forms of "overactivity," such as excessive work or exercise, to help replace activities that might be serving as avoidance behaviors with more carefully considered, value-based activities. Whatever the form PTSD-related avoidance takes, it tends to interrupt life and, over time, contribute to difficulties functioning in relationships or at work.

So What Exactly Is Behavioral Activation?

Let's go over what we mean when we use the term "behavioral activation." The name is actually a pretty good description of the therapy approach; we want to help you *activate* behaviors that represent progressive steps toward living your life according to your values and achieving your individual life goals. Behavioral activation is not simply "doing things" or "being active," but instead, doing things that matter to you. Also, as we said above, you may sometimes need to reduce behaviors that are functioning as avoidance.

In more formal terms, behavioral activation is a present-centered, problem-solving approach that, when used to treat PTSD, doesn't require you to talk about or revisit memories of your trauma. Instead, a behavioral activation approach to recovery seeks to identify *your* specific avoidance patterns and replace them with healthy, chosen alternatives. Further, behavioral activation is primarily focused on first changing your behaviors (versus first changing the way you think about your trauma reaction), with the expectation that changing how you behave will naturally change the way you understand yourself and the world. For this reason, we sometimes refer to behavioral activation as an "outside-in" approach, with the belief that changing your outside behaviors will also help you change the internal thoughts and emotions related to your experience of traumatic event(s). We believe that this focus on first changing behaviors may yield faster changes in the way you experience the quality of life compared to trauma-focused therapies that focus on changing your trauma-related thoughts or feelings as a precondition to improving your ability to function in your life. Since it is likely that your avoidance symptoms are both maintaining your PTSD and causing the most impairment in your life, behavioral activation starts by identifying avoidance behaviors.

So, to sum it up, behavioral activation for PTSD seeks to replace patterns that reinforce avoidance—that is, avoidance related to PTSD—with alternative coping strategies to help you resume activities and lifestyles that are rewarding, pleasant, and personally meaningful. As you learn to replace PTSD-related avoidance patterns with alternative ways of coping, you can develop greater confidence and improve the quality of your life. That is the primary aim of behavioral activation—to help you reclaim your life following trauma and jump-start your recovery from PTSD.

Could Behavioral Activation for PTSD Help Me Deal with Other Mental or Physical Conditions?

Behavioral activation could help you in many different ways, not just as a tool for addressing your PTSD. Depression is very common among people with PTSD, and behavioral activation is already a well-established therapy for major depressive disorder. In fact, our approach is based on a form of behavioral activation therapy used to treat depression. By decreasing depression (a close cousin to PTSD) and improving your mood and outlook, you might find that you have more energy and motivation to address your PTSD.

If you value your physical health but have experienced weight gain or loss of fitness since your trauma occurred, you might set behavioral activation goals to increase your exercise and improve your diet. In this way, your behavioral activation strategies can assist you in feeling better physically, with the expectation that this improvement in your physical health will also help your PTSD improve.

In addition, it is common for people with PTSD to also have symptoms of chronic pain for a number of reasons, including the possibility that their psychological trauma also involved physical injury, as is often the case in motor vehicle accidents (Asmundson, Coons, Taylor, and Katz 2002). Behavioral activation therapy shares many common elements with physical rehabilitation techniques: setting goals, gradually increasing activity, and working around challenges or barriers to resuming important routines.

How Can I Be on the Lookout for PTSD-Related Avoidance Behaviors?

Although the principles and skills of behavioral activation are relatively simple to understand, applying behavioral activation to PTSD can sometimes be more challenging. Some of this challenge comes from the ways in which PTSD-related avoidance can be unintentional and manifest in many different forms of behaviors. Let's revisit the example of Karl to highlight how to identify patterns of PTSD-related avoidance using behavioral activation. As you read the example, make note of specific avoidance behaviors, or patterns of avoidance, that you recognize in Karl's story.

Karl had been separated from the Marine Corps for several years and had struggled with patterns of isolation, heavy drinking, intense episodes of anger (e.g., "road rage"), and an almost constant feeling of being keyed up to the point that he was only sleeping in three- to four-hour blocks of time. He recognized that he would benefit from professional help but kept putting it off, not wanting to stir up memories of his combat experiences.

When he decided to seek out therapy to "give it another chance," he indicated that he had met a woman and really valued the relationship. So Karl was feeling more motivated to "turn it around" than he had been for years. However, he also shared that he worried that he didn't have much to offer someone else, as he had struggled to keep a steady job, gained twenty pounds since leaving the military, and felt "lost" with regard to his future.

Before the Marine Corps, Karl had enjoyed going to the movies (he liked action/ adventure films the most), weight lifting, training in the martial arts, and going out dancing at clubs with his friends. Since returning from his last deployment, Karl found that he felt uncomfortable in movie theaters because people sitting behind him put him "on alert." Karl said that he now only watched movies at home. However, he also shared that he was surprised when he became triggered watching a science-fiction action film. Karl shared, "It was stupid—I knew it wasn't real, but when they started doing battle with the aliens, I kept thinking of Fallujah and started to have a panic attack. I shut off the movie but stayed upset for a couple of days." For this reason, Karl reported that he typically only watched movies he had already seen so that he wouldn't be caught off guard by violent action scenes.

Karl explained that his PTSD symptoms also were interfering with dating, as he was convinced that if a woman witnessed his nightmares or safety-checking behaviors, she would become scared and "dump him." So Karl tended to date women only for short periods of time, typically breaking off the relationships within a few months. However, when he met his fiancée, he admitted that he let his guard down ("I was drunk"). He shared that he was surprised that she seemed to understand how to "tread lightly" around the discussion of his military service. She later shared with Karl that her father had served in Vietnam and had struggled with many of the same issues that Karl was experiencing. Karl reported that, because he felt more comfortable talking with this girlfriend than he had "in years," he was motivated to try and see if he could navigate a longer-term romantic relationship.

Karl's Avoidance Behaviors and Their Costs

As you read through Karl's experiences with PTSD after his military service, could you recognize patterns of avoidance related to his efforts to cope with his trauma-related symptoms? Take a moment to make a list of Karl's avoidance behaviors.

Avoidance Behaviors:

1. _____

2. _____

3. _____

4. _____

5. _____

Did you easily spot the avoidance? Social isolation, patterns of emotional detachment in relationships, alcohol abuse, avoiding therapy, and even anger (to keep people "at bay") are common across people who experience very different types of trauma.

Can you also identify the "costs" of Karl's avoidance patterns?

Costs:

1. _____

2. _____

3. _____

4. _____

5. _____

Unstable employment, loss of sleep, interruption of pleasurable activities such as going to see new movies, difficulty maintaining relationships, the loss of direction, and poor health are also common among people with PTSD.

But Isn't It Natural to Avoid Things That Relate to My Trauma and Seem Unsafe?

Our answer to this is YES! At the time of your trauma event, your impulses toward avoidance were likely very adaptive. It helps to try to get away from or "step back" from traumatic experiences while they are occurring. Natural avoidance during trauma exposure might include trying to flee or escape in order to stay safe, or it might mean going into "shock," becoming emotionally detached or numb, or even having an "out of body" experience (sometimes referred to as disassociation) until the traumatic event has passed. These responses serve to minimize the impact of the trauma. And avoidance of things that remind you of or are conditioned with your trauma is also very common, and understandable. It's "smart" that our brain and body can generalize from one danger to similar threats; in fact, it likely kept our species from extinction. But sometimes our brains and bodies go too far, developing avoidance patterns that become broad, far-reaching, and life-limiting.

Here is an example of how Annie's avoidance had become reinforced and entrenched:

Annie was well aware of her tendencies to avoid situations that triggered her PTSD. In fact, her life had become so routine, structured, and restricted because she was so good at sidestepping her PTSD triggers. She always paid for her gas at the pump and would sit in her car while she filled her gas tank because she found that standing outside triggered trauma memories. She shopped at the same store so that she could quickly find everything she needed, usually during late-night hours to minimize her social interactions with others. Annie seldom put herself in places where she might be introduced to new people because new relationships tended to trigger feelings of hypervigilance, or as Annie called it, "trust alarms." Indeed, most of Annie's behaviors and routines were designed to minimize her anxiety and fear. And because she was so effective at avoidance, she learned that any deviation from these routines caused her stress. In other words, her avoidance was being constantly reinforced: her efforts to minimize deviations from her routine resulted in a decrease in stress, whereas any activities or behaviors outside of her norm caused her anxiety and fear.

In chapter 2, we will review *your* specific avoidance patterns in greater detail; however, the following exercise will help you begin to explore them.

Avoidance/Reinforcement Exercise

Take a moment to identify some aspects of your PTSD-related avoidance and the ways they are reinforced.

When I avoid _____,
(situation)

my avoidance behavior is reinforced because I experience less _____.
(emotion/reaction)

When I avoid _____,
(situation)

my avoidance behavior is reinforced because I experience less _____.
(emotion/reaction)

When I avoid _____,
(situation)

my avoidance behavior is reinforced because I experience less _____.
(emotion/reaction)

Although we have identified PTSD-related avoidance as our primary target in behavioral activation, it is also important to acknowledge that avoidance *works*. With regard to PTSD, avoiding thinking about trauma, avoiding places that remind you of trauma, and avoiding activities associated with memories of the trauma all "work" *in the short run* by reducing your distress. However, over time your life may consequently become more and more narrow and unsatisfying. Avoidance is a little like stopping frequently to fill up a tire that is slowly leaking air; in the moment it allows you to keep going. However, in the long term, you haven't really fixed the problem and you increase the risk of becoming stranded on the road.

In addition, ironically, avoidance can actually lead to more fear and distress over time. This is because each time you avoid a trigger, it confirms your belief that the trigger is dangerous, even though it may only represent a reminder of your traumatic events. The ongoing distress, conditioned to more and more environments that you then avoid, is like the further damage you create by driving on the leaking tire—you are actually increasing the chances of being stranded by not addressing the underlying problem.

This pervasive avoidance associated with PTSD can become entrenched, and then secondary problems can occur as a result of avoidance, like relationship problems (not returning phone calls or texts from friends might result in their "giving up" over time), work or school problems (missed work or classes can lead to low job or school performance, ultimately increasing the likelihood of unemployment or underemployment), depression (limited opportunities for pleasure or meaning makes most of us feel down or depressed), and more chronic and severe PTSD. Thus, pervasive patterns of avoidance can result in larger, global costs that have serious and negative consequences that can disrupt a person's life and interfere with recovery from PTSD. What are some of the larger, global "costs" to your avoidance behaviors?

Costs of PTSD Avoidance to Me

Below are examples of some of the common global costs associated with pervasive PTSD avoidance patterns. **Circle** any areas in your life that are negatively impacted by your tendencies to avoid thoughts, feelings, situations, or people, and list any others that come to mind:

My health	Peace of mind	Friendships	Self-esteem
Romance	Freedom to travel	Job security	Joy
Sex	Hobbies	Confidence	Sleep
Hopefulness	Financial security	New experiences	Relaxation

Other costs:

_____

_____

_____

_____

How Do I Overcome Avoidance Through Activation?

We want you to overcome your habits of avoidance in order to regain some of the positive aspects of living listed in the exercise above. Once we identify which avoidance patterns to target, behavioral activation uses goal setting, planning, attention, and problem-solving strategies to help you overcome your avoidance and work around practical barriers to achieving your life goals. The aim of behavioral activation is to systematically increase your engagement with meaningful and pleasurable activities but to do so in ways that acknowledge and help you overcome the pull of avoidance.

Behavioral activation for PTSD begins by having you determine your goals, based on a careful consideration of your values and the life you want to have at the present time. We will introduce a method for tracking and scheduling your activities and noticing the connection between what you do and how you feel. This process will also help you better recognize your patterns of avoidance.

Sometimes avoidance isn't obvious to you or others because it takes the form of emotional numbness or detachment from your surroundings. If you are busy but simply "going through the motions" of your life, you may be missing moments and experiences that could help improve your mood and progress toward a better life. Because you are "checked out" or "numb," you may not be fully appreciating things that could bring you a sense of satisfaction or happiness. In behavioral activation, we use the term "attention to experience," which is similar to mindfulness and means being present in the moment so as to fully experience the positive or meaningful experiences in your life. We will talk more about attention to experience and mindfulness in chapter 8.

Behavioral activation also relies on active problem solving to help you overcome barriers to engaging in activities that you value. Sometimes this might involve finding a new way to do things that "works around your PTSD." For example, if you and your spouse tend to stay home most nights because you are easily triggered by being out in public settings, it is possible that your avoidance patterns are damaging your relationship (your spouse may get tired of your turning down invitations to do things with other people). You may greatly value your relationship, but your PTSD is calling the shots. It may be that you need to get creative to overcome the "costs" to your relationship associated with avoiding going out in public.

In this example, perhaps you could plan a special date night at home, fixing a favorite meal, planning an activity (e.g., playing a board game), or making a point of discussing topics outside of the usual "day-to-day" issues. This alternative way of working on your relationship goals might reflect the value you place on your relationship and convey to your spouse their importance to you while sidestepping some of the anxiety and hypervigilance you might feel at a restaurant. You might plan a movie night and invite one or a few trusted friends to your home. Alternatively, you could choose to plan a date in public at a relatively quiet and private location, perhaps during a late afternoon when a restaurant might be less crowded. Scheduling a lunch date at off-peak hours might push you outside of your comfort zone a little but also might set you up for a more successful experience than trying to focus on a conversation during the busiest of dinner hours.

We spend more time talking about alternative coping strategies and problem-solving skills in chapters 5 and 7. However, we want you to *begin* to think about ways to overcome avoidance and get nearer to the valued things you are missing in your life right now.

Working Around My PTSD

Take one of the examples of reinforced avoidance you listed in the Avoidance/Reinforcement Exercise and consider what underlying value or experience you miss ("the cost") through your avoidance; then generate a list of other ways you might work around your PTSD to recover the valued parts of your life.

When I avoid _____,
                                    (situation)

my avoidance behavior is reinforced because I experience less _____.
                                                              (emotion/reaction)

The "cost" of my avoidance is _____.

I could try and work around my PTSD and recover aspects of the valued experience in these alternative ways:

Alternative 1) _____

Alternative 2) _____

Alternative 3) _____

Remember, you may have to try out several alternative ways to get back to the valued parts of your life that have been negatively impacted by your PTSD. The important point is that you are taking action toward something you value (e.g., your relationship) and ensuring that your PTSD doesn't dictate your life. And by engaging in meaningful and pleasurable activities, the portion of your life that is defined by PTSD becomes smaller relative to the amount of your life that is determined by YOU. And as you rebuild a richer and broader life outside of your PTSD symptoms, you will likely find that you are better able to cope with your PTSD symptoms as they become less frequent and less intense.

Summary

PTSD can be understood as a "learned" response to traumatic events whereby PTSD-related avoidance is often reinforced, such that disengaging from your life may immediately reduce your stress levels while simultaneously setting you up for a smaller, less rewarding life. Behavioral activation is an effective treatment for PTSD, with potential benefits for addressing other conditions such as chronic pain and depression.

You have embarked on your journey of recovery by beginning to practice identifying avoidance—as well as the long-term costs associated with your PTSD-related avoidance—and to develop some ideas about other ways you might approach situations that you typically avoid. In the next chapter, we will ask you to explore your personal avoidance patterns in greater detail.

CHAPTER 2

Understanding Your Patterns of Avoidance

Now that you have some understanding of the role of avoidance in maintaining PTSD, let's focus on the specific ways avoidance may play out in your life. Before we go further, though, we want to stress that *avoidance is natural and understandable* after trauma, that it might be out of your awareness, and that it's not your fault! But by understanding your avoidance patterns, you are taking the first important step in recovering from PTSD. Take a moment to read more about Annie's avoidance behaviors.

Last year, after Annie was sexually assaulted in a parking garage on a first date, she refrained from parking her car anywhere but on the street. This was practical in some ways, as she was happy to find free parking in some neighborhoods near her favorite stores. It seemed to her that shopping at local places on the main street was better for the community, and when she needed to go to the mall, one or both of her daughters would always accompany her and they would park as close to the entrance as possible. However, she once tried to go to a large movie theater with her kids and was forced to park in an underground garage. While walking to the theater entrance, she could feel her heart pounding, and she had a sense that someone was waiting for her. She grabbed for her daughters' hands and increased her step, making them walk with her to pick up their speed. After this, the fear got worse, not better.

Identify Your Patterns of Avoidance

Sometimes avoidance patterns are obvious to the outside world, for example, social isolation or tendencies to avoid triggers such as crowds or loud environments. Sometimes avoidance patterns can be more subtle, such as drinking alcohol (to avoid the anxiety that comes from being in public) or getting angry and ending a friendship with someone as a means of avoiding future feelings of hurt or sadness.

Avoidance can take almost any form, including sometimes *doing things* that at first seem to be positive or healthy but really function as an avoidance strategy. For example, we've found that some individuals with PTSD engage in extreme exercise routines or high-demand work schedules in order to avoid internal thoughts or feelings associated with their trauma. Although exercise and hard work are generally thought of as positive activities, extreme degrees of either can increase risk of injuries or damage to personal relationships.

Below are examples of common avoidance patterns:

- Not going places or doing things to avoid reminders of traumatic events or because it would feel stressful or unsafe

- Working excessive hours to avoid intrusive memories of traumatic events

- Staying emotionally detached in relationships to try and minimize betrayal or hurt

- Playing video games or watching TV to avoid thoughts of the traumatic event(s)

- Intentionally causing physical pain (punching a wall, cutting or burning yourself) to distract from trauma memories

- Using alcohol or marijuana to decrease the likelihood of PTSD-related nightmares

- Cultivating anger to decrease or avoid feelings of helplessness or fear

Remember, generally people engage in these avoidance patterns for a very simple and good reason—they lead to short-term, immediate relief. And because you usually feel a bit better right after, avoidance patterns are (negatively) reinforced. So it's more likely that you are going to respond the same way the next time you are in the same situation.

Unfortunately, avoidance patterns usually result in greater problems later on because by avoiding something that makes you feel anxious or stressed, you don't resolve the issue (for example, you continue to feel uncomfortable in crowds, have conflicts with others, and so on).

Consider this analogy: You set out for a road trip (life plans) only to experience a car crash from a rock slide (trauma). Although your car still runs, the crash has changed how you drive, making it much more difficult to get to where you had planned. You may avoid driving on roads near hills where rocks are visible, or you may drive far below the speed limit out of caution, which can put you at risk on a highway, not to mention delay your arrival. These changes in your driving can be likened to different types of avoidance in your life. So in the exercises that follow, let's have you consider the various types or forms of avoidance that might interfere with your getting "on the road" to recovery from PTSD. We'll stick to the driving analogy.

Avoiding the Boulders in the Road

Let's start by getting down in writing the situations, experiences, and activities you know you're avoiding, much like we did in the last chapter for Karl. Consider what you no longer do that you used to enjoy (prior to trauma), or things that you'd like to do but don't because it feels too stressful or unsafe or reminds you of your trauma. At this point, try not to censor your responses (for example, because you think something truly is dangerous or because you no longer have interest in an activity; we'll consider these issues later); there is no commitment to do the things you write. This exercise is to help you understand patterns, not change your behavior. For each of these questions, try to think of as many things as you can, but if you come up with only one or two, that's okay; for now, just try to brainstorm.

What did I used to do that I realize I haven't done since the trauma?

_____

_____

_____

_____

_____

_____

_____

_____

What did I once enjoy but now avoid, saying to myself, *Oh, I can't do that?*

_____

_____

_____

_____

_____

_____

What situations, places, or activities remind me of the trauma or actually make me feel as if I'm back in the trauma? (For some readers it may be difficult to think about these things; we invite you to try, but if doing this is too stressful, just skip this question.)

_____

_____

_____

_____

_____

_____

Handling Icy Conditions

Now consider situations you still put yourself in or activities you still do (so you're not really avoiding), but you endure them with a great deal of stress and try to get through them as quickly as possible. We call this "white knuckling." Examples might be grocery shopping by rushing in and out quickly or only going late at night, driving but avoiding any situation with traffic, socializing but leaving as soon as you can and talking to as few people as possible, and so on.

What were the last six things I had to "white knuckle" through?

_____

_____

_____

_____

_____

_____

Being in a Fog

A slight variation to "white knuckling" through something is numbing out or not feeling pleasure or enjoyment when engaging in activities. Consider things you might still be doing, but you feel numb or uninterested at the time, like you're just "going through the motions." (Examples might include spending time with your family but not feeling engaged or happy, going to work but feeling no "drive," being sexually intimate but "checking out," and so on.)

What situations do I do automatically, like a robot?

_____

_____

_____

_____

_____

_____

When did I arrive someplace or leave a situation with no memory of the process of getting there or of what happened (e.g., a meeting, a phone conversation)?

_____

_____

_____

_____

_____

_____

_____

Spinning Your Wheels

Avoidance patterns can involve ways of thinking, such as rumination (repeatedly going over past events) or worry (repeatedly thinking about the future), that can function as internal distractions or efforts to identify and avoid triggers and responses. These types of avoidance patterns may not be obvious to you until you begin to ask yourself why you are thinking about the past (rumination) or the future (worry), only to discover that you are attempting to think yourself out of a past traumatic experience (*If only I had not gone out that night, I wouldn't have been in the car accident*) or anticipate and avoid a future traumatic experience (*If I keep my guard up, I won't let myself get caught in a helpless situation again*).

What are the things that I worry about happening in my life?

_____

_____

_____

_____

_____

_____

What things do I ruminate about from my past?

_____

_____

_____

_____

_____

_____

_____

Driving Under the Influence

Let's continue this self-exploration a bit further. Many people with PTSD find that they are able to engage in activities only if they have items with them that help them feel safe, such as a weapon, anxiety medication (even if they don't take it), or a particular person or people. Some people will engage in activities if they drink alcohol, smoke marijuana, or take other drugs or medications. Consider the kinds of things you may have with you or ingest that help you feel safe or less stressed or afraid (possibly not in all situations).

What things (or people) do I have with me to make me feel safe?

_____

_____

_____

_____

_____

_____

_____

What substances do I ingest to make me feel safe or calm?

_____

_____

_____

_____

_____

_____

Speeding

By now you may be realizing that avoidance is tricky and can show up in a number of different ways. As we said earlier, there is another way that avoidance can manifest that might at first seem to be the opposite of avoiding—overdoing certain activities. It is common for people with PTSD to overengage in some activities, either because this keeps them from doing other activities (that are stressful) or because it helps to distract them from unpleasant emotions or thoughts. Examples include spending the majority of waking hours at work, spending several hours a day at a gym or playing video games, gambling, binge eating (or restricting food)...really any activity that is taking up an unusual amount of time and has negative consequences (for you or people you care about).

What do I overdo?

_____

_____

_____

_____

_____

_____

Getting a Flat Tire

Finally, we'd like you to consider activities you may no longer engage in because of injuries (that may or may not relate to your trauma), physical pain and limitations, or changes in your circumstances. So, you may have no desire to avoid these activities, but because your body or opportunities have changed, you can no longer do them. For example, maybe you used to love to hike and ski but chronic back problems make this impossible. Or maybe you used to love salsa dancing but you live in an area where there are no clubs that offer this. Perhaps you used to be in the military and this gave you structure, purpose, and camaraderie, and you have felt adrift since you left. While you may not be *intentionally* avoiding these activities, the impact of not doing them may be the same—you may be more isolated, more anxious or stressed, and more depressed. By identifying these activities too, we can help you consider alternative activities that may give you some of the same meaning, pleasure, or structure.

How does pain or injury change what I do?

_____

_____

_____

_____

_____

_____

What things do I want to do but am unable to do because of pain or physical limitations?

_____

_____

_____

_____

_____

_____

Understand the Function and Impact of Avoidance

It can't be overstated that avoidance is not your fault and is common after trauma. As mentioned in chapter 1, your brain is wired to move you away from things that evoke painful emotions and sensations. We would have been wiped out as a species a long time ago if that was not the case! Avoidance can keep you safe and out of harm's way. It's also important to know your limits and pace yourself. Sometimes avoidance is useful and healthy if it's in the service of taking care of yourself and preserving your resources for other things and doesn't cause any bigger problems in your life. As you start to consider addressing your patterns of avoidance, it can be helpful to reflect on the short-term and longer-term effects of avoidance. This will help you determine which patterns are most important to address.

My Avoidance Patterns and the Effects

Look back over the avoidance patterns you identified in this chapter. In the spaces below, write down those that are the most frequent or that you think may be impacting your life the most. Then consider the short-term effects (that is, what it does for you, how it helps) and the long-term effects. In most cases, the short-term effects will include feeling better, or not feeling worse. There may be other short-term effects too, such as preventing conflict or rejuvenating energy. For the long-term effects, consider the impact this avoidance pattern has had on your overall quality of life, as well as that of others who are close to you (e.g., family, friends, coworkers). Some types of avoidance may have no significant long-term consequences; therefore, we won't consider those patterns problematic. But before you make that conclusion, we encourage you to really reflect on your life, including what you used to do as well as what you would like your life to be, to see if there might be some significant effects of avoidance. You may even do a little poll of people you are close to, to see if your avoidance impacts their lives in ways you might not be aware of.

Here's an example from Karl:

Avoidance Pattern: *I drink a few beers at night to relax and fall asleep.*

Short-term effects: *I do feel relaxed, and I don't think about my experiences in Iraq as much before bed. I fall asleep easier.*

Long-term effects: *The quality of my sleep isn't very good, I wake up tired. My fiancée would like more quality time together in the evenings and she says she doesn't like how checked out I am when I drink.*

And here's an example from Annie:

Avoidance Pattern: I won't let my kids go on playdates at other kids' homes.

Short-term effects: I feel less worried, less anxious when they are at home with me. I know they are safe.

Long-term effects: My girls really want to be able to go to other kids' homes. They feel they are missing out and it makes them unhappy and frustrated with me. I want them to be able to be more independent and I know I can't keep them at home forever.

Now fill in yours.

Avoidance Pattern: _____

Short-term effects: _____

_____

Long-term effects: _____

_____

_____

Avoidance Pattern: _____

Short-term effects: _____

_____

Long-term effects: _____

_____

_____

Avoidance Pattern: _____

Short-term effects: _____

_____

Long-term effects: _____

_____

_____

Avoidance Pattern: _____

Short-term effects:_____

_____

Long-term effects: _____

_____

_____

Avoidance Pattern: _____

Short-term effects:_____

_____

Long-term effects: _____

_____

_____

What do you notice from this exercise? Does it give you some ideas of the types of avoidance you'd like to address? We also hope you can appreciate the benefits (at least short-term) of avoidance and the fact that not all avoidance is a problem. However, the premise of our approach is that too much avoidance contributes to the development and maintenance of PTSD (and depression) and, if not addressed, can actually grow over time and create bigger problems and difficulties.

The Downward Spiral of PTSD

The following figure shows what the course of PTSD often looks like: a downward spiral. (You can download this figure from the website for this book, http://www.newharbinger.com/43072.)

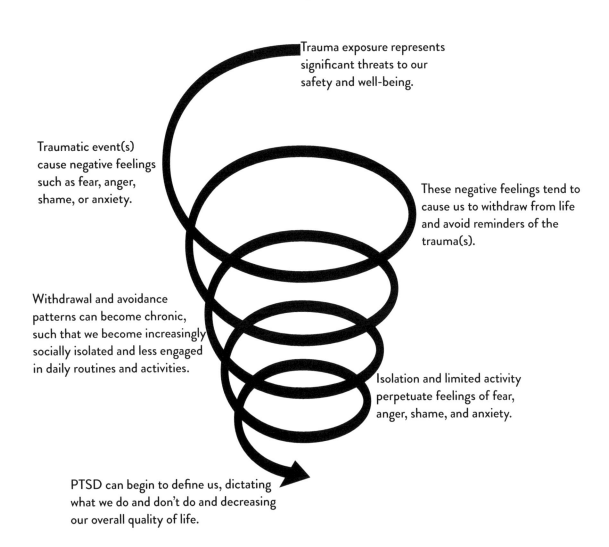

The Downward Spiral of PTSD

Trauma exposure represents significant threats to our safety and well-being.

Traumatic event(s) cause negative feelings such as fear, anger, shame, or anxiety.

These negative feelings tend to cause us to withdraw from life and avoid reminders of the trauma(s).

Withdrawal and avoidance patterns can become chronic, such that we become increasingly socially isolated and less engaged in daily routines and activities.

Isolation and limited activity perpetuate feelings of fear, anger, shame, and anxiety.

PTSD can begin to define us, dictating what we do and don't do and decreasing our overall quality of life.

Am I on a Downward Spiral?

After looking at the figure, consider the following:

Does this make sense in your own life? On a scale of 0–100%, how much does this fit with your experience?

_____

How much has your avoidance grown over time, resulting in additional problems and more severe PTSD symptoms?

☐ Not at all   ☐ A little   ☐ A lot   ☐ An extreme amount

Take a moment to read about Annie's downward spiral, which started after her first experience with sexual assault:

Annie had first experienced sexual trauma during her second year of college. She was at an off-campus homecoming party with her roommate, but she didn't know many other people at the party. After initially hanging back and talking only to her roommate, about an hour into the party Annie struck up a conversation with a member of the football team, a man who later that night would end up assaulting her. After her traumatic event, Annie chose not to share what happened with her roommate and tried hard to "just get past it," but the event certainly impacted her at the time. Annie no longer enjoyed being around others when alcohol was present and would experience anxiety (and sometimes panic attacks) when she was in crowded rooms or around loud music. She mostly spent her time in the library or her dormitory room when she wasn't at class. She even found that she could no longer enjoy football, or other sports, even just viewing it on TV. She started to wear bulky clothes and would start crying "out of the blue," at times when she would look at herself in the mirror. She developed a habit of looking at specific places on her face to do her makeup (eyes only, or hair) but never took a full look at herself and even stopped looking at herself in photographs.

Annie waited several years before beginning to date men. She would become triggered and angry whenever a date would make any references to wanting to initiate sex, often feeling as though this was a red flag that he might be dangerous. She did eventually begin a long-term relationship with a man she met during the last year of her graduate school program. Because he had no interest in organized sports, she felt it was easier to spend time together without getting triggered. Although they became emotionally close, physical intimacy remained a challenging issue for Annie, resulting in infrequent sex. After marrying this man, they became more emotionally and physically distant. They tried to work on their relationship in counseling, and eventually they had two daughters. However, Annie's anxiety and avoidance of intimacy persisted after the births of her children and again became a point of contention in her marriage. She initiated a divorce after five years of marriage as she felt they had grown apart too much and she didn't feel capable of making further changes.

Breaking the Downward Spiral Pattern

Behavioral activation is an approach to help you get active and reengage in your life again, either by resuming activities you used to enjoy and found meaningful before you developed PTSD or by helping you to develop new meaningful activities. It is the opposite of withdrawing and avoiding. As we said, while this is a relatively simple concept, it can be challenging to accomplish. A good portion of this workbook focuses on overcoming the wide range of barriers that may make activation difficult for you.

Here we want to highlight a few key strategies that are important as you move forward with your recovery using behavioral activation.

Take small steps. The approach we'll describe in this workbook involves breaking your goals into small and doable steps, monitoring how you feel after doing these, and building on those steps and activities that improve your overall quality of life. The slow pace may feel challenging to you at times; if you previously were able to function at a high level and were very engaged in life, you may feel impatient and frustrated with how things are now. Small steps may feel too slow or irrelevant to where you want your life to be. But it's what works! Our goal is to help you have successes and really be able to evaluate which actions and activities make a difference for you.

If you have ever tried to push a car out of a muddy ditch (or seen someone else trying to do it), you're probably familiar with the idea that rocking it back and forth in the beginning is key to gathering momentum for the "big push."

That idea is key to behavioral activation for PTSD. Initial steps should be designed to create movement rather than to accomplish the entire goal in one push. So start small but keep your eye on the bigger goal, be patient with yourself as you start, and be mindful of moments when you seem to have some good momentum built so you can really lean in!

By building momentum with small steps toward change, you can avoid overwhelming yourself and build confidence along the way. Remember the quote "A journey of a thousand miles starts with a single step."

Be specific when setting goals. In chapter 3 we will guide you toward setting personal goals for yourself based on your personal values. In general, it is best to set goals that are specific and well defined. For example, rather than setting the goal of "improving my health," consider the specific ways that you would meet that "big picture" goal—perhaps by setting a goal for weight loss ("I want to lose ten pounds in the next six months"). The more precise you are when setting goals, the more likely you are to meet these targets, or at least identify the roadblocks that you encounter and consider alternatives to help you overcome the roadblocks.

Take an "outside-in" approach. Often, we do things when we feel like doing them. There is nothing wrong with that under usual circumstances. If we feel like going to a movie, we go. If we want to talk to a friend, we call them. In behavioral activation we say that is working "from the inside-out" (Jacobson, Martell, and Dimidjian 2001). However, with PTSD, what you feel like or don't feel like doing can be related to fear and sadness, keeping you stuck in the downward spiral. So, in this case, you need to be willing to try some small things that you may not feel like doing; in other words, start from the "outside" and over time it will get easier (the "in"). Feeling anxious or unmotivated is common with PTSD. But in order to break the PTSD spiral, it will be important to commit yourself to trying, even when it is hard.

Our feelings and behaviors are linked, and if we start behaving differently, this can actually change how we are feeling over time. When you change your actions, you are teaching yourself that you can be safe while also pursuing meaningful activities. So the primary goal is to change what you do first, with the expectation that this will lead to changes in how you think and feel.

Practice. Like any new skill, practice is essential. We have found that the more people practice setting goals and taking action steps toward these goals, the more they benefit from this approach. Each week we encourage you to determine concrete steps in the form of specific activities to try, and over time, you can look to see how taking these steps impacts your sense of well-being.

What Patterns of Avoidance Have I Overcome?

You have very likely overcome some patterns of avoidance in your life. Perhaps you didn't realize that was what you were doing. Take an opportunity now to think about how you've already accomplished some of this work. What patterns of avoidance have you overcome in your life (since your trauma or at other times)? How did you do this?

_____

_____

_____

_____

_____

_____

My PTSD Challenges

For this exercise, we have included another illustration of the downward spiral of PTSD that has been left blank to allow you to write your own experience. (This figure is also available on the website for this book, http://www.newharbinger.com/43072.) In the figure, we note the way that behavioral activation can generally help at various points to break the spiral. Take a moment to fill in the blanks with your experience. You might also consider sharing your thoughts and responses to the questions and exercises in this chapter with an important person in your social support network, such as a spouse or close friend.

My PTSD Challenges

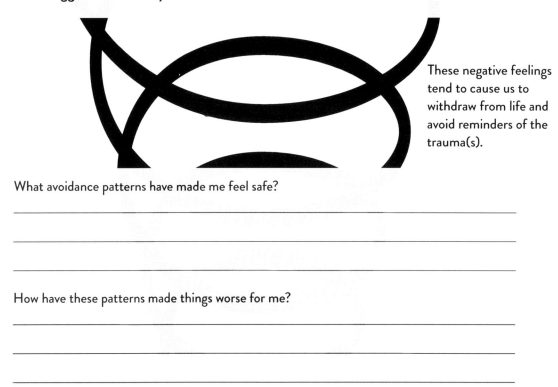

Trauma exposure represents significant threats to our safety and well-being.

What negative feelings have you experienced since this event?

_____

_____

_____

For many people, the process of behavioral activation not only allows them to engage in valued activities, but also frees them from some of the negative feelings that have been triggered in so many situations.

These negative feelings tend to cause us to withdraw from life and avoid reminders of the trauma(s).

What avoidance patterns have made me feel safe?

_____

_____

_____

How have these patterns made things worse for me?

_____

_____

_____

You may also have thought about how you want your life to be different. In the next chapter we'll talk about taking steps toward building the life you want, but here you might make a few notes about the kind of things that would be included in the life you want.

_____

_____

_____

_____

_____

Behavioral activation will help you to act from the outside in, taking small steps, so that you will begin to engage in activities that are important to you but that you have stopped since the trauma. We will break down the steps to allow you to approach situations, people, and places that have felt scary in a way that is manageable and not overwhelming.

How has this all changed me? How has it changed my life?

_____

_____

_____

Behavioral activation is designed to increase your exposure to rewarding experiences and to help you reengage in life. Even if some things need to be different because of physical limitations or changes in life circumstances, in behavioral activation we look for alternatives that will be meaningful and fulfilling.

Summary

Avoidance—a significant factor in PTSD—can take different forms, including behavioral (not doing certain activities), cognitive (rumination or worry), and emotional (emotional numbing, self-medication with substances). PTSD often follows a downward spiral (i.e., the traumatic event leads to negative feelings, which lead to withdrawal and avoidance, which lead to isolation, which lead to a restricted and unrewarding life). In this chapter you identified which types of avoidance are part of your current life and have impacted your downward spiral so that you can begin to target them through behavioral activation.

In the next chapter, we are going to start exploring your values and help you set personal goals for your future. We will break down these goals into concrete steps for behavioral activation. We'll begin by having you consider your values—that is, what matters to you in your life. Behavioral activation is not about simply getting active; it's about moving you forward in the life that you want to have.

CHAPTER 3

Assessing Your Values and Setting Goals

Identifying your values and setting personal goals is critical to using behavioral activation to recover from PTSD. Consider the following analogy: Having PTSD is a bit like getting lost while driving in a big city in rush hour. You may be feeling panicked and have a sense of urgency to speed up to find your route out to escape. However, driving around frantically in different directions to find an escape can actually leave you feeling more lost, more discouraged, and more hopeless. So it makes sense that one of the first things you should do when you are lost is to stop and consider, *what direction should I head in? How will I know if I am moving ahead in a purposeful way* (versus going in circles)? This chapter is designed to help you answer those questions.

Here was Annie's first experience with exploring her values:

Annie was well aware of her PTSD symptoms and the ways in which they had "stolen" the best parts of her life since she was traumatized by sexual assaults. Annie expressed fear that she wouldn't be as effective helping her children navigate the world safely, and as a result, she had begun to isolate herself and her children. Yet, when Annie began to explore her personal values, she quickly identified some of her core beliefs related to her commitment to helping others (as evidenced by her decision to go into social work). She also wanted to provide a safe environment for her two children, and she believed strongly in the importance of fostering a positive community of friends to "get through the tough times" in life. Indeed, watching herself become more socially isolated and less effective at work was causing her to feel depressed and guilty because her actions (driven by her PTSD) were not aligned with her core values. So she began to identify the specific avoidance patterns in her life that were incongruent with these values of service, protection, and community.

Annie shared that simply reviewing these values helped her feel more hopeful and provided her some direction on where to start her behavioral activation toward recovery. She stated a desire to improve her job performance and change the ways she parented her children to allow them to be safe but not scared of the world. She also realized that she wanted to build a community of people who could help her and her children live fuller, better lives.

PTSD as a Barrier to Setting Goals and Moving Forward in Life

As we've discussed, the symptoms of PTSD can get in the way of doing the very things that help to alleviate PTSD, including setting goals for change. Karl's experience exemplifies this.

When we first met Karl, he shared that he had become accustomed to the patterns of a life with PTSD. He couldn't really imagine himself living a rewarding life. In fact, he became nervous when he thought about making changes in his life ("I'm worried that trying to make changes will just bring more pain"). Although he often felt lonely, he was all too familiar with the pain of losing someone close to him—the death of his friend during deployment had "taught" Karl that losing meaningful relationships could cause him years of emotional pain. As a result, he felt that it was "safer" to be lonely than to risk losing another friend or loved one. In fact, years of PTSD symptoms (emotional numbing and detachment in relationships) had made it difficult for Karl to even remember what close relationships felt like—he could only remember the painful experience of grief. Karl could not imagine a future in which he felt close to others…as a result, he became resigned to being alone.

Further, Karl continued to feel guilty about his friend's death. Although part of him understood that he could not have prevented his friend from being killed, he strongly believed that it would have been a better outcome if he had died instead. For this reason, Karl found that he had difficulty prioritizing his own mental health and well-being. Indeed, whenever someone suggested that Karl do something positive for himself, his mind would take him back to the memory of his friend's death and Karl would conclude, I deserve this pain.

Karl shared that he felt lost after he separated from the Marine Corps. When he enlisted, he had a strong sense of purpose and felt that serving his country would give his life meaning. In particular, Karl had noticed that the friendships he had made in the military were especially strong because he and his friends shared a collective sense of purpose. He had also shared many intense and personal moments with the other Marines with whom he served. After his last deployment, Karl felt more confused about the value of his service ("I'm not sure what good it did for anyone") and was more distrustful of the military (or any type of authority). Nonetheless, Karl missed his previous sense of purpose (service to other people) as well as the comradery he had with other Marines, yet he found that it was difficult to replicate these types of relationships in his postmilitary life. Thus, he experienced a tension between what he missed and truly valued about the years he spent in the military (i.e., service, close relationships) and the traumatic memories he held as a result of his last deployment.

Can you relate to Karl's fear of change and his concern that trying to do things differently will bring more stress? PTSD can make it difficult for you to reverse the downward spiral because it can get in the way of you *even imagining* a future different from your current life. In the last chapter, you may have reflected on how narrow or "small" your life has become because of trauma and PTSD. As difficult as it may feel to be confined to this narrow life, we suspect that it has also become familiar. Sometimes, we choose the familiarity of discomfort over the fear of uncertainty, even when the need for change is apparent to us (or others around us).

In addition, PTSD-related avoidance can make efforts to change difficult. Did you recognize the PTSD avoidance symptoms that became barriers to Karl's efforts to set goals and imagine a life different from the downward spiral of PTSD? Karl's PTSD-related avoidance (avoiding feelings of grief and loss) became barriers to setting goals related to his desire to develop new relationships.

The experience of trauma can cause you to lose track of or question your personal values, causing you to feel like a "different person" from who you were before PTSD became part of your life. Not having a clear sense of what you value in life makes it difficult to set personal goals for change because you have no clear direction forward. Did you see how Karl's traumatic experiences impacted his sense of purpose and personal values?

Karl's military traumas had impacted his sense of purpose, and he wasn't sure that his efforts produced any good. His traumas also undermined his respect for authority and made it difficult for him to find a sense of meaning in his postmilitary life.

Did you notice that a significant barrier to Karl's efforts to set goals involved feelings of guilt (he felt deserving of pain)? PTSD may have also caused *you* to feel as though you deserve your current feelings of unhappiness. Remember that PTSD symptoms may include pervasive patterns of self-blame as well as feelings of guilt or shame. Many of the people we have met feel some confusion about seeking out happiness. They of course wish that they felt better, but have also felt as though they earned their unhappiness—often because they believe that they should have somehow been able to prevent the trauma from occurring in the first place. If this is true for you, we will help you practice seeking happiness and observe how "acting as if" you deserve happiness might change your thoughts and beliefs about your right to feel better about your life.

How Does PTSD Impact My Goals?

Take a moment to reflect on ways that your PTSD may be interfering with your personal goals in life. Circle "True" or "False" for the following statements, and then write other ways that PTSD has impacted your sense of yourself or the future.

"I have gotten used to having PTSD."

True   False

If you have become accustomed to having PTSD, how has this impacted your life goals?

_____

_____

_____

"I can't imagine feeling different from how I do right now."

True   False

What happens if you try to imagine a different way of being? Do you experience any fear or anxiety when you try and consider a life without PTSD?

_____

_____

_____

"I would rather be prepared for the worst outcome than be disappointed."

True   False

Does preparing for negative situations actually help you avoid the bad feelings you encounter when you are disappointed? What costs might be involved in bracing for the worst outcome?

_____

_____

_____

"I feel disconnected from who I was before the trauma."

   True   False

How have you changed since you experienced your trauma(s)? Is there some part of you that has remained? Are any of the changes you have experienced helpful to you in your life now?

_____

_____

_____

"I have lost trust in human nature."

   True   False

Can you think of some people in your life who are trustworthy? Are there some situations where you might imagine extending (some degree of) trust?

_____

_____

_____

"I deserve some of the pain I feel from my PTSD."

   True   False

How does the belief that you deserve the pain of PTSD impact your behaviors in relationships?

_____

_____

_____

Are there other ways that PTSD has impacted your view of your future? For example, has it changed your confidence within yourself? Has PTSD made it difficult to imagine a long life? Write down any and all thoughts that come to mind:

1. _____

2. _____

3. _____

4. _____

5. _____

If you identified with some of these barriers to focusing on your future, we want you to recognize that while these thoughts and beliefs are powerful, they can also change over time. Other therapies might have you question and examine these beliefs or change your thinking as a first step to making changes in your life. For many people, this can be a good strategy. However, we are going to propose a different strategy, the type of "outside-in" approach that behavioral activation uses to "test out" these beliefs by *first* taking action toward changing your behaviors and *then* assessing whether these thoughts and beliefs change over time. Admittedly, making changes in spite of your thoughts and beliefs about yourself and the world can feel like a leap of faith. But in our experience, once people start to make changes in their behaviors, they begin to see that some of the barriers—both internal and external—they perceived to recovery begin to feel less true.

Figuring out where to start this change process can feel overwhelming. We recommend that your goals for activation be determined by and remain aligned with your personal values. This may mean that you resume activities that you previously enjoyed before you developed PTSD. This may require some problem solving and trial and error, but we feel confident that you can reclaim important parts of your life.

In addition, the change and growth process might mean that you need to develop new routines and begin new activities. Many of the people we have helped use behavioral activation for PTSD have discovered routines, hobbies, and approaches to relationships that they had not known would make them happy. In many ways, this can be the most exciting part about using behavioral activation—you get to discover new ways to live your life that reflect your values and bring you a sense of purpose and meaning.

Because your personal values are the primary guide to starting your activation toward recovery, let's take a few moments to have you explore your own values.

Exploring Values

Personal values can have a big impact on our lives, providing guidance in our daily lives and helping to define our sense of who we are and what types of activities are most meaningful to us. Values can be broad, such as "honesty" or "loyalty," or specific, such as good health or deep connections with family or friends. We have listed some examples to help you start thinking about your own values. Remember, there aren't right or wrong values—rather, each of us gets to decide what constitutes a high-quality life.

Examples of Personal Values

Providing financial security to myself and/or my family

Contributing to my community (e.g., volunteering, being a good neighbor, or helping to maintain safety)

Having a good work ethic

Being loyal to my friends or family

Improving/increasing my relationships (friendships, family relationships)

Pursuing new experiences, adventure, or travel

Becoming and/or staying physically healthy

Setting time aside for relaxation and leisure

Pursuing personal growth

Committing to my spiritual or religious practices

Improving my education and/or occupational status

Cultivating self-compassion and/or compassion toward others

Being active in political matters

Fostering appreciation and gratitude

Being active in my children's school and/or extracurricular activities

Improving and/or maintaining my personal living environment (home, yard)

Below we are going to invite you to reflect on your values. It is important to take your time with this and consider that your values may be different now than they were previously—this happens with life experiences—even (or especially) traumatic experiences. Try to have an open mind and really consider what would make your life meaningful and enjoyable at the present time.

Note: Oftentimes we become focused on areas that we sense are "supposed to" be important to us, or areas that *other* people think should be important to us. However, with behavioral activation for PTSD, we do not promote doing things simply out of a sense of obligation. Rather we encourage you to prioritize things that really matter to YOU!

What Are My Values?

(You can download and print a copy of this exercise at http://www.newharbinger.com/43072.)

Now take a moment to reflect upon *your* values, and list the top five values that are central to who you are or who you want to become.

1. Value: _____

    Where did you learn this value? _____

    Has it changed since you developed PTSD?   ☐ Yes   ☐ No

    If so, how did this value change after your trauma(s)?

    _____

    _____

2. Value: _____

    Where did you learn this value? _____

    Has it changed since you developed PTSD?   ☐ Yes   ☐ No

    If so, how did this value change after your trauma(s)?

    _____

    _____

3. Value: _____

   Where did you learn this value? _____

   Has it changed since you developed PTSD?   ☐ Yes   ☐ No

   If so, how did this value change after your trauma(s)?

   _____

   _____

4. Value: _____

   Where did you learn this value? _____

   Has it changed since you developed PTSD?   ☐ Yes   ☐ No

   If so, how did this value change after your trauma(s)?

   _____

   _____

5. Value: _____

   Where did you learn this value? _____

   Has it changed since you developed PTSD?   ☐ Yes   ☐ No

   If so, how did this value change after your trauma(s)?

   _____

   _____

Using Your Values to Determine Your Goals for Behavioral Activation

Now that you have spent some time reflecting upon your personal values, let's use these values to further clarify your personal goals. We will start with some initial "big-picture" goals and then help you work backward to find the "first step" actions that you can take to begin to achieve these goals.

Here are some examples of "big-picture" goals and the values they represent:

"Big-Picture" Goal	Value
Be more involved with my children	Family
Be more productive at work	Pride in my work ethic
Spend more time doing hobbies	Leisure
Be promoted to manager	Having authority

What Are My "Big-Picture" Goals?

(available at http://www.newharbinger.com/43072)

Ask yourself, *What are some areas of my life that represent my values and that I'd like to improve?* This question will lead you to determine your big-picture goals. These initial target goals should have the potential to increase your sense of happiness or represent meaningful aspects of your life. It is also helpful to link the target goal to the value that it represents.

Aim to have these big-picture goals represent different values or areas of importance. For example, rather than choosing to set three different goals related to health (e.g., increase fitness, improve diet, take a daily multivitamin), we encourage you to target separate domains of your life (e.g., increase my fitness for health reasons, improve my relationship with my spouse, and volunteer my time to help out others in my community).

Keep in mind that it will be important to prioritize some of these because they are meaningful, even if they aren't immediately enjoyable. For example, you may not enjoy housework, but if you highly value a clean living environment, completing chores might turn out to be meaningful to your quality of life.

"Big-Picture" Goal	Value

It might be helpful to rank your big-picture goals from most important to least important.

Now that you have identified meaningful areas to target, identify the most important value you wish to prioritize as you begin behavioral activation. Ask yourself the following questions. (If you have more than one high-priority value, answer the following questions for each of your core values.)

What makes this value meaningful or important to me?

_____

_____

_____

How might my life be different if I were living my life according to this value?

_____

_____

_____

How near or far do I feel I am from living my life according to this value?

_____

_____

_____

In what ways have I acted on this value most recently? How has it been similar or different compared to before this time?

_____

_____

_____

Breaking Big-Picture Goals into Smaller, More Immediate Goals

Now that you have identified your values and some big-picture goals, you'll need to consider identifying some smaller goals that will help you ultimately achieve these big-picture goals. For example, let's say that you first identified the big-picture goal of improving your physical health. Now we need to further refine the big-picture goal into some type of objective outcome. The big-picture goal of improving your health might get translated into a smaller, more immediate goal of increasing the number of hours you exercise each week. We are getting closer to a starting point, but even so, you might wonder, *Where do I begin?*

For many people, the objective outcome goal of increasing exercise time can get muddled because it is easy to try a number of different approaches only to find that it is hard to be consistent or to keep track of what is working and what is not. For this reason, we encourage you to identify very concrete steps, or "action steps," you might take to reach that objective goal. (In chapter 6, we'll explore how to pace yourself with action steps, but here we'll focus on identifying initial action steps.) As you identify action steps that you might take toward your goal, in this case increasing your exercise hours, also consider potential barriers that might interfere with your steps toward increased exercise.

For example, if you set the goal to improve your health through regular exercise, you might identify the following first-step action items:

1. Pick a type of exercise that you think you'd enjoy (e.g., walking, running, lifting weights, playing basketball).

2. Look through your current clothes to see if you have appropriate workout clothes (e.g., shorts, athletic shoes).

3. Look at your weekly schedule to find days and times that you could set aside for working out. (Remember to start small! Even ten to fifteen minutes of activity can help you build momentum toward establishing an exercise routine.)

4. Troubleshoot: are there any obstacles or challenges you might encounter as you try to add in exercise to your weekly routine? If so, what can you do to help reduce this barrier? For example, you might need to set your alarm clock earlier in the morning if you are someone who has difficulty waking up to get going for the day.

5. Determine whether there are smaller steps you might take toward this goal.

6. If you aren't sure what type of exercise you might most enjoy, read some books or online material describing common types of exercise.

In our experience, people sometimes get stuck early in the process because they focus on the multiple things they will need to do to ultimately meet their objective goals and they begin to feel overwhelmed or discouraged. Nevertheless, these first steps are critical to creating some momentum toward change. So do your best to stay focused on each initial step forward.

Keep the following considerations in mind when determining first action steps:

- Your PTSD symptoms may have been present for months (or years or decades) and it may take some effort and time to restart your life; be patient with yourself as you make initial steps toward change.

- Related to this idea, it is often best to make *very* small steps toward your personal goals to ensure that you can make realistic commitments to change. If any of your first-step action items feel too difficult, break them down into even smaller steps.

- Consider asking someone close to you for ideas or support to help you determine how to best initiate these first steps. Sometimes, simply telling someone what you plan on doing to start moving toward a goal can improve the likelihood that you will complete it (e.g., telling a friend that you are planning to start walking for exercise on your lunch break or inviting them to join you).

The key to using behavioral activation for PTSD to restart your life is to build up momentum over time. Remember, even taking these initial small steps can be challenging, and PTSD can try and pull you back down the spiral. However, small steps become bigger steps, and then we establish routines that ultimately can redefine our lives. If you keep trying, you can eventually overcome the pull of the PTSD spiral and reclaim your life!

Here is a description of Karl's initial action-step plan that he used to begin his behavioral activation toward recovery from PTSD.

Karl had identified his big-picture goals for behavioral activation as (1) improving his relationships with others—in particular, his fiancée—and (2) improving his physical health by resuming weight lifting.

Karl decided that a first-step action item would be to begin to plan weekly "dates" with his fiancée, with the understanding that they would choose activities that they both enjoyed and that would allow them time to talk and interact with one another. His fiancée was very pleased that he had initiated the idea of planned activities that would allow them to feel more connected to each other. Karl proposed that they go for a hike in a nature area near their home because he felt that he would be less anxious and "on guard" in that setting (versus going to a crowded restaurant). Although his primary aim was to target his relationship, he was also aware that going for a gentle hike would serve his goal related to physical health. After Karl discussed this plan with his fiancée, he added it to his phone calendar, picking a day and time when he knew they were both available for several hours.

Karl also scheduled first-step actions to help him advance his other goal. He decided to set aside an hour to do some Internet research to find a nearby gym that was affordable and that offered twenty-four-hour options, since he knew that heading into a crowded gym at peak hours would not likely be a positive experience. After finding two different options, he also realized that he could take an action step toward this goal by driving by each gym during nonpeak hours to look at the location and to get a sense of how many other people he might encounter should he join and restart weight lifting.

Did you notice how Karl identified first-step actions by considering his values and anticipating potential challenges to achieving these goals? This is important because, especially in the beginning, you want to set yourself up for success by starting small and planning ahead.

Now let us help organize your action steps to start your activation toward recovery. Review the following suggestions to get started:

- Pick the big-picture goal that feels like a priority in your life and consider first-step actions that you might make in the next week to get started.

- If you feel confident that you can complete this action item, consider adding one to two more action items that represent different big-picture goals. Note any action items that represent more than one goal or value—these are often some of the best targets for behavioral activation, as you get to make progress in multiple areas of your life!

- To improve your chances of success, choose first-step action items that can be easily completed in less than one hour and enter into a calendar (e.g., on your cell phone) the day and time that you'd like to complete this action item.

- Be sure to anticipate and problem solve any foreseeable challenges and obstacles that may impede your completion of the action item(s).

- When you are in the midst of completing your action item, pay attention to how it feels to be working toward this big-picture goal. Also notice how completing the action item might influence your mood during and after you stop the activity. Be especially mindful of any distractions you might experience while doing the activity.

- If you fail to complete any of your action items, pay attention to what interfered with their completion. Did you encounter any practical barriers that you hadn't anticipated? Can you identify any PTSD-related avoidance that might have made it challenging to try out the new activity?

Summary

PTSD can interfere with goal setting and disconnect you from your personal values. To begin to address this, you have identified some important personal values that might help you set behavioral activation goals for your recovery from PTSD as well as some initial first steps toward these goals. In the next chapter, we address some of the difficulties that may arise when you've identified values and goals and broken them into steps. We'll review some of the triggered response and avoidance patterns, or "TRAPs," that PTSD can create as you begin activation. We'll also introduce you to some strategies to help identify PTSD-related TRAPs in preparation for developing alternative ways of coping with PTSD-related barriers to your recovery. Identifying these TRAPs will be key to maintaining progress toward your personal goals.

CHAPTER 4

Tracking Your Activities and Looking for PTSD-Related TRAPS

Very often, PTSD symptoms can get triggered when you are trying to make changes in your life. These triggered responses will often prompt you to return to old patterns of avoidance, potentially taking you off stride as you try to advance toward new ways of living your life. If you are not careful, these patterns of responding to internal or external triggers keep you in the downward spiral of PTSD and serve as what we call PTSD-related "TRAPs" (Jacobson et al. 2001), making it challenging to make progress toward your big-picture goals.

To identify TRAPS, we will teach you to look at avoidance in the moment. You have learned that avoidance leads to more avoidance and pulls you away from rewarding activities, so we want to help you recognize when you are in that TRAP and how to get out of it. You know that there are several consequences of avoidance, and that it can be both helpful (e.g., avoiding a car crash by stopping at a red light) and detrimental (e.g., avoiding going to the dentist because you once had a painful dental procedure). We experience our lives in moments and in episodes. Knowing the big picture—in other words, understanding general situations where you are likely to avoid—and knowing how avoidance keeps you from pursuing value-driven goals is important. However, the best way to keep moving toward behavioral activation is to regularly practice to identify and overcome avoidance patterns in the moment.

Identifying TRAPs

We use the acronym TRAP or TRAPs in behavioral activation to help us identify these invitations back to the downward spiral of PTSD. TRAP(s) stands for Trigger, Response, Avoidance Pattern(s). See descriptions of each below:

- **Trigger**—something that occurs either internally or outside of us in the environment that we have a response to (usually a negative response for our purposes). Examples include having a nightmare or daytime memory of a traumatic experience, feeling unsafe because of something that reminds you of your trauma(s), or being startled by an unexpected noise or movement.

- **Response**—the impact that the trigger has on you, such as feeling stressed, angry, sad, or on guard.

- **Avoidance Pattern(s)**—the common ways people respond to these painful emotions, for example, withdrawal from the world, use of drugs and alcohol, emotional numbing, or interpersonal detachment.

In some ways, your TRAPs describe how PTSD shows up in your daily life. Emotional or physiological reactions in response to reminders of traumatic events are intrusive symptoms of PTSD. These come about because of the learned conditioning that paired the traumatic event (and your emotional responses at the time) with certain sights, sounds, smells, or situations that you currently encounter. The avoidance patterns that follow triggered responses represent PTSD avoidance symptoms and typically function to create distance between you and the memories and emotions associated with the traumatic event.

Now we want to help you increase your awareness of your specific PTSD triggers and emotional responses, as well as the specific ways that you tend to respond to these triggered responses. Below are some common examples of triggered responses.

Examples of PTSD Triggered Responses:

Anxiety (response) to violent movies (trigger)

Shame (response) in response to discussions of childhood sexual abuse (trigger)

Anger (response) when feeling helpless (trigger)

Grief (response) on the anniversary (trigger) of a loved one's accidental death

Sweating and racing heart rate (response) to images of a natural disaster (trigger)

Stomach pain and diarrhea (response) while driving past the scene of a previous car accident (trigger)

Depending on what types of trauma(s) you have experienced, you may have triggers that differ considerably from those described above. A combat veteran might become triggered in response to physical geography that reminds her of the arid and hot conditions in Iraq. A person who has a history of sexual trauma might become triggered by images or language depicting sex or romance. You may also encounter different triggers and responses across various situations: the triggers you encounter out in public may be different from the triggers you experience at home. Sometimes triggers are subtle or indirectly related to a trauma memory, such as having a positive emotion (e.g., a moment of happiness) that seems unconnected to the traumatic event but that can still prompt a PTSD response.

Take a moment to read about Karl's description of his triggered responses. See if you can identify some of the avoidance patterns specific to these triggers.

Karl noticed that over several particularly hot days during one summer week, he began to feel angry for no reason he could immediately identify. However, it reminded him of the anger he felt during his deployments, and he realized that the hot weather was in fact a reminder of his military service, causing him to recall the uncomfortable heat of Iraq. The level of his anger during his deployment wasn't a surprise to him then…he often would put himself into an aggressive mindset on days his unit went out for patrols. But now in the civilian world, and during this week of looking for TRAPs, Karl realized he was "revving up" by becoming angry when he left his house.

During that same week, Karl became upset and tearful after hearing a heavy metal song on the car radio that he had listened to repeatedly during his deployment. This surprised him because he had loved listening to the song to "get pumped up" while in Iraq but now felt a wave of sadness. In fact, once he noticed this, he came to realize that he had mostly stopped listening to the metal music when he was driving (instead playing classic rock or country music). Karl began to reflect on how his taste in music had changed since his deployment and became frustrated that his PTSD had such a "long reach" into his life. He had in essence stopped appreciating a whole genre of music because of his PTSD, and he resented that his military service had cost him the freedom to listen to songs that he had previously enjoyed.

At night, Karl had trouble sleeping because of worry patterns late at night. In fact, it seemed that his mind would go looking for things to worry about when he was preparing to go to bed for the night. There was something about the quiet of his apartment at night that he found unsettling. In Iraq, Karl had found out that civilians would often leave the scene of an ambush before it happened, assuming that they had been "tipped off" ahead of time. The quietness of situations where Iraqi life seemed to stop became a red flag for danger. Now, as his apartment became quiet, he noted that he would become anxious and "on alert." Rather than feel anxious, Karl had unconsciously developed a habit of trying to "think ahead" to identify potential stressors, and he would begin to develop plans for how he might handle these stressors. However, the "cost" of this late-night worry was his sleep! Although thinking about how he might handle stressors seemed to help him prepare for them, it also left him feeling too keyed up to sleep, and he would often not fall asleep until the early morning hours. Further, the limited sleep he was getting contributed to his daytime irritability, and he often felt even more reactive on days when he had only slept three to four hours the night before.

What Are Karl's TRAPs?

Can you identify Karl's TRAPs in the example above?

1. Trigger: _____

    Response: _____

    Avoidance Pattern: _____

2. Trigger: _____

    Response: _____

    Avoidance Pattern: _____

3. Trigger: _____

    Response: _____

    Avoidance Pattern: _____

Identifying your own triggers can be challenging because identifying them will likely put you back into some sort of awareness of your trauma(s). However, keep in mind that identifying your PTSD triggers and anticipating the types of responses that follow can help improve your sense of control over your PTSD. Ultimately, we want you to be very tuned into your PTSD triggered responses so that you can prepare yourself for when you encounter them and then *choose* how you'd like to respond over time, making the triggering situations less powerful.

What Are My Triggers and Responses?

(available at http://www.newharbinger.com/43072)

Take a few moments to think about your recent triggers and list the responses you experienced in the **past two weeks.**

Situations, people, places, or things that have recently triggered my PTSD:	My responses to these triggers:
Example: Karl's hearing heavy metal music on the radio	Example: Karl became tearful and started to remember his combat experiences.
1.	
2.	
3.	
4.	
5.	
6.	
7.	

Triggered responses can range from unpleasant to terrifying. However, the parts of PTSD that truly undermine a person's ability to live a high-quality life often show up in the forms of avoidance patterns. As we've noted, avoidance patterns can take many different forms (remember the "Avoiding the Boulders in the Road" and "Spinning Your Wheels" exercises?) and might be harder for you to identify than your triggered responses. When you think about the impact of PTSD on your daily life, can you identify the TRAPs? What about identifying both the immediate benefits to these TRAPs as well as the longer-term costs associated with avoidance patterns?

What Are My Avoidance Patterns?

(available at http://www.newharbinger.com/43072)

Now go back over your list of recent triggers and responses from above. Consider how you might have engaged in avoidance following these triggered responses.

Trigger	Response	Avoidance Pattern(s)
1.		
2.		
3.		
4.		
5.		
6.		
7.		

Daily Activity and Mood Monitoring

Finding TRAPs is at the heart of behavioral activation. But some avoidance patterns aren't always easy to identify right away. First, we want to ask you to start paying more attention to how you are spending your time. Tracking your activity and mood is a helpful habit to develop because (1) it can increase your awareness of the connection between what you are doing and how you feel, and (2) you can see what you are *not* doing and identify windows of time that you might try to make changes in your routines.

When asked, "How was your day?" most of us tend to skip over the details of how we feel and spend our time. You may find that you are prone to forget or minimize "good things" that happen to you and instead focus on stressful experiences. This may be in part why you may also struggle with depression and feelings of hopelessness—you may only be noting the challenges and not counting the rewarding moments in your life. You might also spend your time in ways that have a negative impact on your mood, though you might not recognize this at the time. Paying close attention will help you notice the impact.

In addition, it is common for people with PTSD to remain "triggered" for an extended period of time after a stressful event or reminder of their traumatic memories. So, you may be having a triggered response that is influencing your mood many hours (or even days) after the trigger occurred. It can be helpful to monitor these extended responses because they can influence how we experience other events (e.g., feeling angry and frustrated with others later in the day because of a PTSD triggered response that occurred in the morning).

To help you monitor your activities and mood, find a way to keep track of the activities that you are doing during specific blocks of time over the course of your days and week, and how these activities affect your mood. For a while, keep track of everything you do, even the apparently unimportant activities, like sitting and watching TV, as you might notice important information about how what you do (or don't do) affects how you feel. In addition, rate your mood on a scale of 0 to 10, with 0 being not strong at all, and 10 being the strongest you can imagine.

Karl agreed to keep track of his activities over the course of a weekend—and the results surprised him.

Karl's Weekend Daily Activity and Mood Monitoring Chart

Time	Saturday	Sunday
6A–8A	Activity: *Wake up, eat breakfast* Mood: *Contented 8*	Activity: *Sleep* Mood: *NA*
8A–10A	Activity: *Running errands in town-dump, etc.* Mood: *Cranky 5*	Activity: *Awake in bed-nightmare* Mood: *Angry 6*
10A–12P	Activity: *Shopping at big box store and yard supply* Mood: *Angry 5;* *Impatient 10*	Activity: *Little spat with fiancée* Mood: *Frustrated 6*
12P–2P	Activity: *Waiting for Rx. Long lines at car wash* Mood: *Angry 8;* *Irritable 10*	Activity: *Taking a walk* Mood: *Anxious 6; Angry 9*
2P–4P	Activity: *Driving home* Mood: *Annoyed 9*	Activity: *Watching race with a/c on* Mood: *Interested 1; Irritable 9*
4P–6P	Activity: *Home with a/c on* Mood: *Irritable 2*	Activity: *Dinner* Mood: *Bored 9*
6P–8P	Activity: *In bed thinking* Mood: *Worried 5*	Activity: *Cleaning up from dinner* Mood: *Irritable 4*
8P–10P	Activity: *Playing video games* Mood: *Bored 2*	Activity: *Watching TV with fiancée* Mood: *Irritable 3*
10P–12P	Activity: *Getting ready for bed-thinking about tomorrow* Mood: *Worried 3*	Activity: *Getting ready for bed* Mood: *Irritable 1*
12P–2P	Activity: *Sleep* Mood: *NA*	Activity: *Sleep* Mood: *NA*

When Karl looked over his monitoring chart, it became clear to him that his anger was both a response to his PTSD trigger and also a contributor to other problematic situations. Karl noticed that when he was angry, people tended to stay clear of his path. Karl noted that being angry in public helped him avoid interactions with others but also "cost" him a great deal. For example, he worried that he was becoming "the clichéd angry veteran," and he didn't want to perpetuate the stereotypes of combat veterans he had seen in movies and on TV, although he felt like he couldn't help grousing under his breath at the box store. He also noticed that the anger he felt during the hot days carried over at home, making his interactions with his fiancée more "tense" despite the fact that they weren't arguing about anything in particular. Finally, Karl's anger was impacting his health. His doctor had noted high blood pressure, and he would often get tension headaches on days when he felt particularly angry.

Using anger as an avoidance strategy is similar to driving fast; it may get you where you want to go, but you end up missing the details of the journey and increase the chances for a collision. Keeping your "engine" revving fast will also cause you more stress over time and can negatively impact your physical health. So Karl's use of anger made sense but also took a toll.

Now it is your turn. Below is a form that we often share with our clients when using behavioral activation. (A blank copy of the Daily Activity and Mood Monitoring Chart is located in the appendix of this workbook and on the website for this book, http://www.newharbinger.com/43072.) We encourage you to use this over the next week to keep a record of your activities and how you are feeling during these blocks of time. The purpose is to jot down reminders for self-monitoring purposes; it doesn't need to be detailed. If this paper version feels inconvenient for you to use, you could also utilize electronic calendars (e.g., the calendar on your cell phone or computer) or explore phone apps designed to help track your mood and activities. Whatever form you use, we strongly encourage you to fill this out in "real time," recording your actions and feeling states several times throughout the course of the day. Record the specific activity you are engaged in and your mood, along with a rating (for example, "a little sad" might be rated 3 out of 10). Finally, at the end of each day, review your chart to identify any TRAPs that might have occurred and make note of the "costs" of your avoidance patterns on those days.

Daily Activity and Mood Monitoring Chart

Time	Mon	Tues	Wed	Thurs	Friday	Sat	Sun
6A–8A	Activity Mood	Activity Mood	Activity Mood	Activity Mood	Activity Mood	Activity Mood	Activity Mood
8A–10A	Activity Mood	Activity Mood	Activity Mood	Activity Mood	Activity Mood	Activity Mood	Activity Mood
10A–12P	Activity Mood	Activity Mood	Activity Mood	Activity Mood	Activity Mood	Activity Mood	Activity Mood
12P–2P	Activity Mood	Activity Mood	Activity Mood	Activity Mood	Activity Mood	Activity Mood	Activity Mood
2P–4P	Activity Mood	Activity Mood	Activity Mood	Activity Mood	Activity Mood	Activity Mood	Activity Mood
4P–6P	Activity Mood	Activity Mood	Activity Mood	Activity Mood	Activity Mood	Activity Mood	Activity Mood

6P–8P	Activity Mood	Activity Mood	Activity Mood	Activity Mood	Activity Mood
8P–10P	Activity Mood	Activity Mood	Activity Mood	Activity Mood	Activity Mood
10P–12A	Activity Mood	Activity Mood	Activity Mood	Activity Mood	Activity Mood
12A–2A	Activity Mood	Activity Mood	Activity Mood	Activity Mood	Activity Mood
TRAPs during the day	1. 2. 3.	1. 2. 3.	1. 2. 3.	1. 2. 3.	1. 2. 3.
Costs of Avoidance					

My Daily Activities and Mood

To get started with activity monitoring, pull out the Daily Activity and Mood Monitoring Chart and try to reconstruct yesterday up until right now. Once you do that, think through when you will complete this over the coming week; our suggestion is once a day at a minimum; the more you can do it during the day, the more accurate it will be. Keep it up—this too is behavioral activation!

After you've completed the Daily Activity and Mood Monitoring Chart for several days or a week, reflect on these questions.

What did I notice while completing this activity and mood rating form?

_____

_____

_____

_____

Were there any patterns I observed between the types of activities I am doing and how I am feeling?

_____

_____

_____

_____

Could I see any open spaces in my days where I might start to add new activities (or resume activities I used to do)?

_____

_____

_____

_____

Below is a description of Annie's observations from her first week of activity and mood monitoring. In particular, she noticed that her triggered responses tended to build upon one another, so that one tended to increase the magnitude of the next one.

Over several weeks of monitoring her activities and moods, Annie noticed some patterns emerging. She noticed that she often woke up feeling anxious and unsettled, especially after the many nights when she had experienced a nightmare about her sexual traumas. She also noticed that, on these days, she was more irritable and tended to "snap" at her daughters as they were getting ready for school. She had always felt nervous sending them "out into the world," but mornings seemed to be the hardest part of the day regarding these worries. Annie's daughters, sensing her irritability, tended to talk less about their upcoming day and the things they had planned after school (Annie wondered if she was actually wishing they would stay quiet, because talking about their upcoming day tended to cause her to worry more about their safety). Annie also noticed from her daily monitoring that once she arrived at work, she felt better. She tended to "jump in" to her work, which she found helped distract her from her worry about her daughters. Also, if she had experienced a nightmare the previous evening, being busy at work helped her forget about the images she had experienced while sleeping. Work made her feel so much better that she found that she tended to "overdo it," often taking on too many projects or clients to the point that she would be exhausted at the end of the day. This stood out to Annie as she logged her work hours into the daily monitoring chart and began to think about the short-term and long-term "costs" of her excessive work regarding her health and her relationships with her children.

We encourage you to keep up your daily monitoring for the rest of time that you are using this workbook so you can track your progress and review old and new patterns to support your use of behavioral activation. Keeping a daily log helps you identify your TRAPs and can be a powerful way to motivate you to act and take steps to overcome your PTSD. It's possible that you may have difficulty noticing TRAPS if your life is fairly restricted by avoidance. We expect that, as you begin to make changes in your life and pursue big-picture goals, PTSD-related TRAPs will frequently arise. Be patient with yourself during this stage of change. By increasing your awareness of these TRAPs, we hope you can start to appreciate what a powerful force PTSD can be in your life. In the next chapter, we are going to discuss strategies you might use to break avoidance patterns and cultivate new, alternative ways of coping in response to PTSD triggered responses.

Staying Motivated!

When you first begin to track your activities, moods, and TRAPs, it can feel overwhelming. You might notice how prevalent your PTSD avoidance symptoms are in your daily life and begin to feel discouraged by the high "costs" you identify along the way. It is similar to the sinking feeling you might have when your car engine begins to make alarming noises and you take it into the mechanic, bracing yourself for the estimated cost to repair the vehicle. We bring this up because initial reactions of feeling overwhelmed or discouraged are not only normal but, with the appropriate perspective, can also be a powerful tool to keep you motivated. Many of our clients who have shared these reactions have found it helpful to step back and reflect on their larger mission to recover from PTSD. As Karl said, "It's not like I can just go out and buy a new life…this is the one I have and I'd rather rebuild it into something that makes me happy than go through the world complaining and disappointed by how PTSD has impacted me in the past."

Here are some points to consider that may help you remain focused on making the kinds of changes in your life that will bring you satisfaction and happiness.

- The awareness you are developing will give you greater ability to manage your PTSD symptoms. Knowledge gives you the opportunity to make changes in how you respond to your symptoms.

- The avoidance patterns you identify have "worked" to some degree, or you wouldn't be using them. However, avoidance patterns often have high "costs." By looking at the TRAPs and their costs, you are giving yourself the opportunity to find new ways of managing your PTSD that are better aligned with your values and goals.

- PTSD is a powerful thing, but you have survived your traumas and (since you are reading this book) you are working toward recovery. This is the type of resilience that will carry you forward toward a better life.

So do your best to maintain curiosity (rather than shifting into discouragement or self-blame) about what hasn't been working so you can be purposeful in your efforts toward change and recovery!

Summary

At this point, you have begun to monitor your daily activities and the moods you experience during these activities. You've also started to practice identifying TRAPs as they arise in your day and note the impact of the TRAP on your mood as well as the "costs" associated with your avoidance patterns. We encourage you to continue to keep track of your daily activities and moods, both as a tool for finding TRAPs and also as groundwork for you to begin to see opportunities to add in meaningful activities to your daily life. We also want to help you stay motivated to make the kinds of changes in your life that will lead to your recovery and a better quality of life. In the next chapter, we will discuss ways that you can turn TRAPs into opportunities to practice alternative coping strategies to help manage your triggered responses and get your life back on track.

CHAPTER 5

Getting Your Life Back on "TRAC"

Now that you have spent some time learning how to identify the TRAPs in your life caused by your PTSD, we want to help you shift your focus toward *changing* these avoidance patterns. Behavioral activation for PTSD helps you get out of the TRAP and get back on TRAC(k). TRAC stands for Trigger, Response, Alternative Coping (Jacobson et al. 2001). The TRAC acronym is used to help you replace TRAPS with alternative ways of coping so that you can reset your life on a path toward recovery. Alternative coping represents your best efforts to find new ways of handling your PTSD-related triggered responses.

Tips to Help Foster Change

To help you prepare for making these changes, we'd like to first offer some important pointers about change. First, change isn't a one-time process. If it was, then most of us would be healthier and happier each year by the end of February because we would simply make a New Year's resolution and stick with it! If you belong to a gym, you are probably familiar with seeing an influx of new members in the first two months of a new year, only to find it thins out as time goes by. So rather than a one-shot approach, change is more likely going to be a back-and-forth process of sometimes trying something new and sometimes going back to your old patterns before you more consistently use new strategies to cope with your PTSD. Don't be discouraged by this…it is how most people alter habits and form new ones.

Second, try and keep a "mechanic's mind" approach to this process. A good auto mechanic learns to enjoy challenges and tries to remain open to the possible reasons why a car engine isn't working. When you think like a mechanic, you expect that things won't go exactly as they should, as is the case when a car doesn't work. Mechanics also can occasionally get frustrated when their attempts fail and the engine still doesn't work. When using the TRAC strategies, try and remain curious about why something doesn't work and why something else does. This means minimizing self-judgement and instead looking for the "why" when you notice yourself engaging in old patterns. This is like the mechanic, who—after having tried several fixes and getting a little frustrated that the engine still doesn't turn over upon ignition—does not feel guilt, but simply takes on the task of trying another solution.

This curiosity is also helpful because, as humans, we tend to predict what will and won't work for us, often without actually trying it out (or experimenting with when and how something might be helpful); so keep an open mind when trying new approaches or revisiting coping strategies that might have worked in the past that you no longer practice. Not succeeding every time, getting frustrated, and needing to try several different strategies are all common experiences when trying to manage difficult emotions or make behavioral changes. Hopefully the frustration will cue you to calmly step back and rethink the plan—like the mechanic, who takes a little break when frustrated and then attempts a different fix rather than give up and throw a wrench across the shop.

Finally, involving other people in this process can help your efforts toward change. Talk to a friend or family member about your efforts to change how you respond to your PTSD triggers. Let the people you feel closest to know you'd like their support as you make these changes. This support might take the form of emotional support (for example, encouragement or participating in an activity with you) or suggestions or advice on new ways of coping. However, although it may be very helpful to observe (or ask) others how they choose to cope with stress reactions, the best alternative coping strategies are the ones that work for *you* and reflect your own personal values. We encourage you to try and balance a stance of openness to new ways of coping with the confidence that only you will ultimately know what helps you cope best with your PTSD and move forward with your life.

Time to Get on TRAC

Let's start off with an exercise that revisits your values and goals; these will serve as an anchor for change to occur.

Getting on TRAC with My Values and Goals

Take a moment to recall some of your previous work to identify your personal values and goals (chapter 3). What are the most important values you hold in your life?

_____

_____

_____

Now think about some of the situations that have been TRAPS for you. Write down one that pulled you off target of acting according to your goals.

_____

_____

_____

Getting your life back on "TRAC" means stepping toward your valued goals in the face of triggered responses, which is the opposite of avoidance. This often will require you to develop a large set of alternative coping strategies to tolerate and manage your PTSD-related responses in specific situations. Sometimes the alternative coping strategies might simply involve keeping your focus on your goals and riding out your initial responses. Other strategies include distraction techniques (e.g., directing your attention to something different in your environment) or "grounding" exercises that might help you come back into the present moment or reconnect with your body and senses. Sometimes alternative coping strategies might entail using effective communication skills, such as learning how to actively listen to others or developing the ability to be assertive when asking for what you need or want from a situation. Often, a good alternative coping strategy might involve seeking out emotional support from a trusted friend or family member in the moment or moments following your triggered responses (we provide a fuller list of options below).

Alternative coping strategies will work best when they both help you cope with your triggered response and are aligned with your personal values and individual goals for recovery. If you can see in the moment how your alternative coping is helping you to get closer to your goals, is value-based, and keeps you from falling into a TRAP, this will increase the chances that you will get traction and stop the wheel-spinning patterns that PTSD creates.

Getting Out of a TRAP and Getting on TRAC

You likely have tried some types of alternate coping in your efforts to manage your PTSD. Think about the TRAP situation you wrote about above, and consider one alternative behavior that might have gotten you out of the TRAP and back on TRAC. Write some notes about how it reflected your values and why it worked (or didn't):

_____

_____

_____

_____

_____

_____

Here's an example of going from a TRAP to being on TRAC:

- **Trigger**—having an intrusive memory of a traumatic experience

- **Response**—feeling stressed, angry, or sad because of the images and feelings associated with the trauma memory

- **Previous avoidance pattern**—drinking alcohol to change emotions and blur the memories of the traumatic event

- **Alternative coping**—rather than resorting to drinking alcohol, deciding to go for a brisk walk somewhere peaceful (in line with your values and goals related to health and wellness) until your body and mind calm themselves without alcohol

Notice that taking a walk may still be a form of avoidance, but, unlike using alcohol, walking represents an example of value-driven behaviors. It is also important to note that it may seem difficult to imagine substituting something as simple as taking a brisk walk instead of using alcohol to avoid intrusive trauma images. You might immediately find yourself saying in your head, *That won't work* or *I've tried that…it doesn't help.* Keep in mind that taking the walk was helpful because it was a value-driven behavior, in line with goals about health and wellness. If taking a walk was just something to do, it might not be as helpful.

So as you consider alternative coping strategies for yourself, reflect on both what could help you manage your reactions *and* what would be consistent with your values and how you want to live your life. Avoidance is almost always more effective in the short run (that's why it's so common!), but getting in touch with your longer-term goals and values will likely make your alternative coping strategies "work" better overall. For this reason, even if you've tried things in the past that didn't seem to "work," we want to encourage you to try again, now armed with this perspective. We also encourage you to try multiple alternative coping strategies until you find ones that work well for you in the right situations. This may take some experimentation to find the right alternative coping strategy for different types of triggered responses.

For example, if taking a brisk walk still leaves you flooded with trauma-related emotions and mental images, it may be that you need to find another coping strategy, that is consistent with your values, for this particular situation. Perhaps you might try calling a friend to help distract you from the images or even talk with the friend about the experience and ask for his support (rather than reach for alcohol). You might also consider putting on some relaxing music or watching a favorite TV program or movie to help you reset your mood. Of course, it would be hard to generate a list of alternative coping strategies to try in the moment; once triggered into a "fight or flight" mindset, it would be hard for *anyone* to generate new ideas on how to cope differently.

Below is a list of positive alternative coping strategies that we have seen work for individuals with PTSD. It is by no means an exhaustive list, but it might help you start to think of what types of activities might work for you.

Positive Alternative Coping Strategies

- Practice deep breathing (breathing in fully, holding your breath for a moment, then releasing) for three to five minutes

- Walk in a mindful way (paying attention to the sensations of each foot placement; attending to the sights, sounds, and smells in your environment as you walk)

- Color in an adult coloring book (also a good way to practice mindfulness)

- Do a house chore you need or want to accomplish (for example, yard work or cleaning up your living space)

- Listen to a guided meditation tape/recording

- Listen to some relaxing music

- Practice prayer or mantra repetition

- Read a fun fiction book

- Watch a favorite comedy show

- Spend time with friends or family (to distract)

- Spend time with a favorite animal or pet (for comfort and distraction)

- Talk with a close and trusted friend or family member about your triggered response

- Write down your thoughts and observations about your emotional reactions

- Engage in a favorite hobby (such as sewing, woodworking, cooking, or baking)

- Exercise (walk, run, stretch, or lift weights)

- Spend time sitting in nature

- Make a cup of tea or coffee

- Volunteer to help a friend with a task

- Volunteer for a cause you support

- Take a shower or bath

- Get a haircut

- Sing or play a musical instrument

- Go for a relaxing drive (if you feel safe doing so)

- Look up places you would like to travel to see

- Read about a topic of interest (for example, history or art)

Keep in mind that finding the right alternative coping strategy for each situation might take some trial and error. The point is for you to break out of the TRAPs that have interrupted your life path and start to experiment with other ways of managing your PTSD.

To maximize the likelihood that you will reach for a new way to cope with PTSD triggers when you need to, we want to guide you to generate a list now (when you aren't triggered). Again, it's helpful to link the alternative coping strategies to a personal value to increase your motivation to try it out when you are triggered. Finally, it may be helpful to take some notes as you try out the various coping strategies so that you keep track of the various triggers and responses and the effectiveness of each alternative coping strategy compared to your past avoidance patterns.

Common Types of Triggered Response(s) and Avoidance Patterns

In this exercise, we'll give you an example of a common trigger, common responses, and previous avoidance patterns that Annie described, and ask you to write about your own.

Common Trigger:

Annie: "I've noticed that seeing movies or reading articles related to sexual trauma will often remind me of my own traumatic events. When news stories started covering topics related to date rape on college campuses, I fell into a funk that lasted months. Now, I am beginning to feel encouraged by the 'Me Too' movement but I also find that reading about these instances of sexual harassment or sexual assault is a huge trigger."

Now You Try It. What is a common trigger that brings up memories of trauma for you? (Choose something that isn't the most distressing for these early exercises.)

_____

Common Responses:

Annie: "I tend to either feel panicky or anxious, or I become embarrassed and ashamed...I get flushed or stiffen up. I get flooded with images of my first experience with sexual assault. Sometimes I even feel like it's happening again...like I'm nineteen years old again and I can sometimes even smell the cologne the guy wore, even though I know that the smell isn't really there."

Now You Try It. What is your common response?

_____

_____

_____

Previous Avoidance Patterns:

Annie: "In situations like this, when I get triggered, I tend to withdraw from people and activities. I go directly to work and directly home. People invite me to do things and I make up excuses to skip out. But then, when I'm finally alone, I start to focus on my traumatic memory and the negative self-talk begins: *Why didn't you see that coming? Is there something about me that invites bad things into my life?*"

Now You Try It. List a couple of your avoidance patterns.

_____

_____

_____

Next, we want you to start making a list of alternative coping strategies. But first, let's look at an example of Annie's TRAC strategies—she grouped each set of alternative coping strategies according to a core personal value.

Annie's Alternative Coping Strategies

"Here are some things I can try instead of withdrawing after I'm triggered."

Value: Health and Wellness

1. I can go for a walk in a peaceful or familiar (safe) area.

2. I can make a healthy snack or plan a delicious meal for dinner.

3. I can practice yoga or stretching exercises.

Annie's Notes: "It seems like I benefit from walking or stretching early in the day but later, when I'm tired, I'm less likely to use these to cope. Planning dinner is helpful because it's something I need to do anyway, but linking it to my values and goals related to health helps me feel like I'm making my life better, not just getting through each PTSD trigger."

Value: Relationships and Social Support

1. I can call a friend or talk to a family member to distract my mind.

2. I can call a friend or talk to a family member to share my struggles.

3. I can spend time with my kids, ask them about their day and what's going on in their world.

Annie's Notes: "When I'm really shaken up, spending time with my kids can be a mixed bag. If I'm distracted or irritable, I end up feeling like I'm not a great mom and that tends to make me feel worse. But I know I can call my sister because she has also experienced sexual trauma and she really 'gets it.' In fact, by sharing some of my struggles with her, we've become a lot closer in the last year. I think we are helping each other, which makes it easier for me to reach out to her when I need her support."

Value: Personal Growth and Spirituality

1. I can write down some of my thoughts or responses to the trigger to help me understand it better.

2. I can engage in prayer.

3. I can attend a church service or read scriptures.

Annie's Notes: "I sometimes have to wait awhile before I can write out my thoughts about a triggered response because I'm still 'in it' and not really good at putting words to paper…but when I do this after I've calmed down a bit, I find I really get a lot out of it. It's like I replay the triggered response in my head and that allows me to prepare better for the next one. So if I'm really triggered, I start by asking God for his love and support…that calms me down so that I can start to reflect on what just happened."

Now you try this process.

My Alternative Coping Strategies

Taking Annie's example, and using the examples you came up with in the previous exercise, write some alternative strategies, grouped according to at least three core personal values. Just as Annie wrote some notes to herself that served as good reflections on her own behavior, and wrote some instructions for herself, we want you to do the same. Having some brief notes can provide encouragement when you feel that using an alternate strategy is difficult.

Rather than engaging in _____(one or more of your TRAPs),
I can instead try out the following alternative coping strategies.

Value: _____

    List three alternative coping strategies aligned with this value.

       1.   _____

       2.   _____

       3.   _____

Your Notes: _____

_____

_____

_____

Value: _____

    List three alternative coping strategies aligned with this value.

       1.   _____

       2.   _____

       3.   _____

Your Notes: _____

_____

_____

_____

Value: _____

    List three alternative coping strategies aligned with this value.

       1.   _____

2. _____

3. _____

Your Notes: _____

_____

_____

_____

Karl's Alternative Coping Strategies

Take a moment to read about Karl's experiences using and refining the TRAC exercise to try to break out of his PTSD-related TRAPs.

Karl had found that the TRAP/TRAC exercises were very helpful. He was now often catching himself in the midst of TRAPs (i.e., when they were occurring instead of after the fact). So he felt ready to begin to try and make some changes and develop alternative ways of coping with his PTSD triggers. For example, Karl was now very aware that summer heat would often trigger his combat memories and that he would in turn become irritable as an avoidance strategy to put distance between himself and his memories of being in combat. He made a list of alternative coping strategies associated with his core values around finding "serenity" and strengthening his relationships.

With his value of serenity in mind, Karl had tried meditation and listening to music. Finding a tolerable (not "too cheesy") mediation recording helped, but only when he was alone. The presence of other people was still distracting. Karl also tried out what he called the "dialed-in listening" strategy to align with his value of strengthening relationships. For Karl, this meant he would ask the person he was spending time with a question and then would try and actively listen to the person's response. In order to actively listen, he paid close attention and then briefly paraphrased the response to make sure that he'd understood correctly and to keep himself focused. Sometimes he would ask simple questions like "How are you doing today?" but he found that most often people would only give one- to two-word answers. So instead he began to ask people more detailed questions (depending on the situation and his comfort at the time).

My Alternative Coping Strategies—Extended

(available at http://www.newharbinger.com/43072)

Now we want you to create an even *larger* list than you wrote in the earlier section, based on your own values, and to try them out. The larger the list you generate, the greater the likelihood that you will find something that works for you in the moment! Above, we provided examples of Annie's alternative coping strategies (three per value category) and encouraged you to create your own list. Now think about even more value categories and more alternative coping strategies. The longer and more elaborate the list, the more likely it is that you will find something that helps you cope with a particular triggered response in the moment. We also recommend that you keep the list of alternative coping strategies on hand (perhaps make the list on your smartphone or take a picture of the list to have as a resource when you are out of your home). This way, you can simply go down your list of alternative coping strategies and experiment.

Value: _____

Alternative Coping Strategies:	When did you try these out? (What were the triggered responses?)
1. _____	_____
2. _____	_____
3. _____	_____
4. _____	_____
5. _____	_____

How did they work for you? What was helpful and what wasn't helpful?

_____

_____

_____

_____

Value: _____

Alternative Coping Strategies:	When did you try these out? (What were the triggered responses?)
1. _____	_____
2. _____	_____
3. _____	_____
4. _____	_____
5. _____	_____

How did they work for you? What was helpful and what wasn't helpful?

_____

_____

_____

_____

Value: _____

Alternative Coping Strategies:	When did you try these out? (What were the triggered responses?)
1. _____	_____
2. _____	_____
3. _____	_____
4. _____	_____
5. _____	_____

How did they work for you? What was helpful and what wasn't helpful?

_____

_____

_____

_____

Value: _____

Alternative Coping Strategies:	When did you try these out? (What were the triggered responses?)
1. _____	_____
2. _____	_____
3. _____	_____
4. _____	_____
5. _____	_____

How did they work for you? What was helpful and what wasn't helpful?

_____

_____

_____

_____

Value: _____

Alternative Coping Strategies:	When did you try these out? (What were the triggered responses?)
1. _____	_____
2. _____	_____
3. _____	_____
4. _____	_____
5. _____	_____

How did they work for you? What was helpful and what wasn't helpful?

_____

_____

_____

_____

Value: _____

Alternative Coping Strategies:	When did you try these out? (What were the triggered responses?)
1. _____	_____
2. _____	_____
3. _____	_____
4. _____	_____
5. _____	_____

How did they work for you? What was helpful and what wasn't helpful?

_____

_____

_____

_____

What did you notice as you generated your list of alternative coping strategies? Were there times when a particular strategy worked and times when it didn't? Remember, the more you make notes about when and how something helps you cope with triggered responses, the more quickly you'll be able to develop a sense of what will work in a particular moment.

Finding alternative coping strategies that help you *advance* toward your goals allows you to both cope with your PTSD reactions in the moment and also build upon your efforts to advance your life. With this in mind, consider ways to repeat or advance your alternative coping strategies over time so that you can create new habits and routines.

Combining TRAC Strategies with Goals

Annie was particularly good at combining her TRAC strategies with her goals for her future. In this exercise, you will read about how she did this and then try to do the same with your own values and goals.

> *Annie had originally listed her priorities for change in accordance with her personal values around relationships. So by the time she was developing new TRAC strategies, she was naturally gravitating toward using strategies that would help her strengthen her relationship with her two children and cultivate new friendships. Annie tried to use one or more relationship-building coping strategies every day.*

Now You Try It. Consider your *highest value(s)* (like Annie's value of having good relationships). Write about a goal that is important to you and how it represents your highest value(s).

_____

_____

_____

Annie worked with another woman at the hospital who she felt might be a potential friend. They were both managers and talked in general terms about their stress at work. Annie began to initiate these discussions more often (instead of waiting for them to happen). Although Annie felt a bit awkward reaching out to her coworker when she felt triggered at work, she learned that her coworker was very receptive to her efforts to seek support. She had assumed that her coworker would find this to be a burden, but instead her coworker began to reciprocate, asking to meet for coffee on "tough days" and sharing more details about both work and home-life stress. This allowed Annie to begin to share more details about some of her safety concerns regarding her daughters and the struggles she experience with her "workaholism." This made Annie feel like the relationship with her coworker was more balanced in a "give and take" sort of way. In her previous attempts to make friends, she worried that her PTSD had meant that she couldn't trust anyone again, but she found that the more she shared about her emotional responses with her coworker, the more she felt emotionally safe. Feeling safe, as well as being more "present" with her children, made Annie feel like she had something to offer others in terms of relationships, which made her feel more confident and increased her self-worth.

Now You Try It. List one alternative coping strategy that you can use when you recognize that you are in a TRAP that helps you gather momentum and *advances* you toward your goal.

_____

_____

_____

Annie noticed that if she tried to stay focused on the moment, she could more quickly "come back" from a triggered response. She also learned to find different levels of engaging with her kids. At the end of the night when she was tired, she would often make some popcorn and snuggle with her kids while watching a movie. On the weekends when she had more energy, she would try and find activities they could do together to refocus herself after a PTSD triggered response. During opportunities to have deeper conversations, she would ask her kids about their friendships, their current interests, and their own goals for the future. Over time, she noticed that her kids were being more open with her, sharing details about their day and interactions at school. This helped her feel like a good mom and also made her feel more confident that if something stressful was going on for her girls, she would know about it.

Now Reflect: When have you practiced alternative coping? What new habits might you be building that are bringing your life back in line with your values?

_____

_____

_____

You can see how Annie began to build new habits around relationships and use these relationships to both cope with her PTSD triggers and begin to make progress on her personal goals. You have also been reflecting on how you are beginning to build new habits. Now that you have used the exercises in this chapter repeatedly over a few days or weeks, take a moment here to write about how things may be changing and may be beginning to look to you like a new, healthy habit.

_____

_____

_____

Summary

Give yourself a well-deserved pat on the back. Already you have developed a list of alternative coping strategies that are in line with your values, practiced using them, and took notes on how they worked in order to compare and contrast which TRAC strategies work best for you and in what situations. Those are big steps. In the next chapter, we are going to talk more about how to pace yourself when making changes to ensure that you are making steady progress without overreaching and setting yourself up for setbacks.

CHAPTER 6

Pacing Yourself to Make Incremental, Strategic Action Steps

At this point, you have identified your personal values and life goals that define (for you) a good quality of life. You have also learned to identify TRAPs that might send you back down the spiral path of PTSD and to practice TRAC strategies to find alternative ways of coping with triggered responses. In this chapter, we want to help you find the right pace for taking "action steps" and moving ahead with your recovery. This is an important consideration because moving too fast can sometimes sabotage efforts to make changes in life, whereas failing to make steady progress can leave you open to falling back into old patterns of avoidance and inertia. Which of these pacing challenges do you think you are more prone to fall into?

My Pacing Challenges

Take a moment to consider the following questions.

Are you more likely to become impatient with your pace of making changes or to struggle to get going?

_____

_____

_____

_____

When you have made progress toward change, what has helped you maintain the pace of change over time?

_____

_____

_____

How will you know if you are trying to move too fast (or are moving too slowly) toward your goals?

_____

_____

_____

Taking on Too Much Too Fast

Let's begin by focusing on the problem of taking on too much too fast. In our work, we see this quite frequently. Oftentimes, once people identify their goals and values, they feel an urgency to jump in and can take on too much. This is understandable, because once you examine all the ways in which PTSD has taken you off track in life, you might desire to make changes quickly to "catch up" with what your life might have been if PTSD weren't present. You might also be aware of how quickly or easily things came to you in the past and expect that same pace of change now. Yet the impulse to take big steps forward can cause problems in several ways.

Problems with Overreaching

There are four main problems with taking on too much too fast. Let's explore each problem, how it can play out, and how you might address it.

PROBLEM 1: MINIMIZING THE IMPACT OF PTSD

As we discussed earlier, avoidance is understandable with PTSD. Likely, there are many activities you no longer do because doing them would bring up strong feelings (like anxiety, fear, or anger), elicit memories of your trauma, or seem unsafe. In your efforts to get your life back you may underestimate or minimize the challenges of approaching these types of situations and activities (perhaps thinking you "should just be able to do it"), jump in full-throttle, and quickly find yourself overwhelmed. This can lead to hasty retreats and confirmation of beliefs that you can't or don't want to do the activity.

One of Karl's goals was to return to a regular weight-lifting routine. He valued health and wellness and had enjoyed weight lifting in high school before he entered into military service. He had also regularly weight lifted while he was in the military, both before and during his deployment. In particular, he found that lifting weights was a useful way to manage his stress. He therefore thought resuming weight lifting would be a good place to start his behavioral activation. He joined a gym and decided to go after work. However, he was immediately stressed when he saw so many people there. He felt like he couldn't get his bearings, and everyone seemed like a potential threat. In addition, he had strong memories of his buddy who was killed during his deployment—they had often lifted weights together. Karl did a few reps and then left, feeling discouraged and frustrated with himself.

Reflecting on Overreaching Problem 1

Consider the following questions regarding the problem of minimizing the impact of PTSD.

In what ways have you underestimated the impact of PTSD symptoms in your efforts to reengage in your life?

_____

_____

What might be some ways Karl could slow his pace but still move forward with his goal of resuming weight lifting?

_____

_____

What insights does this give you into how you might slow your pace but still pursue a goal- or value-based activity?

_____

_____

It is important to remember that changing PTSD-related responses takes time and new experiences. The more you engage in activities without feeling overwhelmed and without other negative consequences, the easier it will get. As we said previously, some discomfort is to be expected when you start behavioral activation, but careful pacing will keep discomfort from escalating and becoming unbearable.

Karl decided to start going to the gym at a less crowded time and to initially only stay for thirty minutes. He would practice paying attention to his experience (for example, the feel of the weights in his hands, the movement of his body) to reduce his focus on other people. In addition, he spent some time thinking about how to navigate the possibility that he would again be triggered to think of his friend and experience grief. He devised an alternative way of coping: rather than avoiding lifting because of grief, he would focus on the positive qualities of this friendship and hold the thought that he could honor his lost friend by getting back into a weight-lifting routine. His friend, who had always helped Karl push himself in the gym, could again serve as a positive motivating factor.

PROBLEM 2: INSUFFICIENT PLANNING/PREPARING

When you begin to activate toward your life goals, you may not yet have fully developed the problem-solving skills, alternative coping skills, or habits of attending to your own patterns of behaviors, so first steps are likely not going to be as successful as you would like. Imagine you are hoping to take a long, cross-country road trip because you value adventure and exploration. Eager to get to your destination, you leave without fueling up the car, checking your directions, or planning for problems that might arise, like flat tires or road delays. If you encounter any of these challenges early in your trip, you might become frustrated and overwhelmed by the distance you have yet to go, increasing the likelihood of turning back. Even if you press on, you might stop enjoying the adventure of the trip because your mood spirals and you begin to think the trip is a stupid idea. Many people who try and make changes in their lives fall into these TRAPs (either giving up or becoming discouraged and devaluing their goals).

Take Annie, for example. One of her primary goals was to allow her daughters to have more independence and time with their friends. When her older daughter was invited to a sleepover, she agreed, knowing it was an important step toward her goal. However, after she dropped her daughter off she realized she hadn't reminded her to pack a toothbrush and hadn't asked the friend's parents what time she should pick her daughter up in the morning. She also worried she hadn't talked with her daughter enough about what to do if she needed anything, and she regretted not thinking to ask if there were firearms in the house and if so, how they were secured. Annie became highly anxious and slept poorly the whole night, convincing herself that her daughter should not have gone on the sleepover.

Reflecting on Overreaching Problem 2

Consider the following questions regarding the problem of insufficient planning.

Rather than prohibit her daughters from going to sleepovers, what could Annie do next time to feel better prepared for future sleepovers (or outings) her daughters have?

_____

_____

_____

_____

What is an example of an activity you have tried that didn't go as well as you hoped because you didn't prepare or plan sufficiently? How might you try again by preparing more ahead of time?

_____

_____

_____

_____

Remember, too, that even with planning, unforeseen obstacles might arise that get in the way of your behavioral activation plan. It's impossible or unrealistic to plan for everything. Like a skillful skier or tennis player, keep yourself flexible and adaptive to what comes and recognize that every step is a movement closer to your ultimate goals.

PROBLEM 3: NOT ADJUSTING FOR THE PRESENT MOMENT

If you are trying to resume activities you used to do, a common problem is trying to picking up where you left off. Many of our clients have expressed frustration to find themselves feeling as though they are "back to square one" when it comes to picking up activities that they had previously enjoyed. By overreaching in your attempt to resume previous levels of activity or engagement, you might find yourself stepping into a TRAP. Discovering you're no longer able to perform the activity at your previous level might trigger frustration, thoughts about your PTSD and its impact on your life, and recalling of details of the trauma. This might set off the same types of avoidance patterns that you are trying to break away from and interrupt your path toward recovery.

The first few times Karl did make it to the gym, he was disappointed by how much strength he had lost. When he tried to push himself to lift the same amount of weight as before, he became worried that he might injure himself. And he was so sore the following day that he felt that going to the gym again the next day (or even several days afterward) would be a disaster. Indeed, Karl's point of reference for his weight-lifting routines was outdated; he had last regularly lifted almost ten years ago, when he was still on active in the military. It seemed hard to imagine how he would ever get back to the habits he had once had.

It's important to consider the range of factors that may interfere with resuming an activity where you left off. As we mentioned under Problem 1, PTSD-related symptoms, including longstanding patterns of avoidance, will make many activities more difficult. Likewise, if you've been struggling with depression, you're working against lack of motivation, low energy, and strong feelings of inertia. Other factors to consider are reductions in physical strength (as was the case for Karl), lack of practice (like for a sport, instrument, or any skill-based activities), physical pain or limitations (if you've had an injury), different life circumstances (for example, having a busier job, kids), and low self-confidence. All of these are *understandable reasons* why you might struggle now at the same pace or intensity that you participated in an activity before your trauma and call for *starting slower*, to overcome patterns of avoidance and develop new routines, strength, stamina, and confidence.

Not only had the past ten years of TRAP habits caused Karl to lose habits of self-discipline, but it was also much harder for him to find the time to work out. When he was on active duty, he lived on a base and his job required him to meet physical standards. He had a number of close military friends on base whom he lifted with and who pushed him to work out, even on days when he felt less motivated. Now he was working a full forty-hour week at a physically taxing job with a construction company. At the end of a workday, he seldom felt like spending another two hours lifting at a gym. Also, he expected that his fiancée would protest because she often complained that they didn't spend enough time together during the week as it was. He considered canceling his gym membership. His efforts to create some traction toward his health goal had now become another TRAP!

Reflecting on Overreaching Problem 3

Below, write down your observations regarding Karl's inability to adjust to the present moment and suggestions for alternative strategies for Karl.

Observation(s)	Suggestion(s)

Reflect for a moment on factors in your life that may make it an understandable challenge to resume (or add a new) activity at the pace, frequency, or intensity at which you might have done things prior to your trauma. What are those factors?

_____

_____

_____

How could you structure the activity to take into account these factors and increase the likelihood that you'll have successes and not become overly discouraged?

_____

_____

PROBLEM 4: HEADING DOWN THE WRONG ROAD

Perhaps most important, you might find that your goals change as you begin to make progress toward them. In our experience, it is very common for people to find that what they thought they valued or wanted in their lives shifts as they begin to activate toward recovery. As much thought as you put into your values and the aspects of your life that you wish to change, it is impossible to know if these are truly your priorities until you set about making changes. You might discover that the things you thought were most important and valuable when you began this process turn out to be less of a personal value and more likely dictated by what others might think is important. You might also find that you decided to return to a value or life goal that you had before the PTSD downward spiral took hold of your life, only to find that you have changed as a person and no longer value or want to accomplish the same things in life. In other words, you might set out on your trip across country thinking that you should stop at national parks and monuments because you enjoyed visiting them when you were younger (and because they are the destinations most often listed in guide books), only to find that what you really like is the experience of finding small towns and visiting with the local people who live there. If you push hard to visit Mount Rushmore, you might miss all the local communities that you might have enjoyed seeing along the way.

Our suggestion here is that you stay open to the (likely) possibility that your goals may change as you take steps with behavioral activation. And rather than view this as a setback, consider what you've learned from your experience and the path you'd like to take next. This is the ultimate road-trip experience!

Finding a Manageable and Effective Pace

Finding strategies to overcome pacing challenges can take many different forms. Even if different people decide to try the same pacing strategies, what works for one person might not work for another. That said, we have outlined several different pacing strategies that might be worth trying out.

Before you take a big step, cut it in half (and if that doesn't work, cut it in half again). Expect to start with small steps and move forward from there. As we mentioned in chapter 2, if you've ever tried to get a car unstuck from snow or mud, you know that giving a big shove rarely works; the wheels just spin. Instead you will have a greater chance of success if you start with small rocking motions and push harder over time. Likewise, if you find yourself spinning your wheels when trying to take an action step toward your long-term goals, consider cutting the step in half. For example, Karl had an out-of-date reference point for his lifting routines (two hours per day, six or seven days per week). Instead of starting with this regimen, he might have started with the goal of going to the gym for thirty minutes at a time, three days a week. He might also have recorded what his ultimate weight-lifting goals were formerly set to be and cut those in half. For example, if his former goal was to bench press 250 pounds, he might set his initial goal at 125 pounds, deciding to cut that again if it proved to be too heavy. He then might slowly move back up to his target weight goals but in five- to ten-pound increments over the course of several months.

Cutting My Goals in Half

Think about any of your behavioral activation goals in which you took on too much too fast. Can you imagine "cutting it in half" and trying smaller steps toward your ultimate goal? What would that look like? What about cutting it in half again?

_____

_____

_____

_____

_____

Experiment with taking steps on different days or times to see what works best. Taking an action step might be easier on some days, or times of day, than others. Experiment with different windows of time to see what works best for you. For example, Karl had originally planned on going to the gym after work each day. However, he found that he was often too fatigued at the end of a work day to feel motivated to lift weights, and it was too crowded. After experimenting with getting up early in the morning to make it to the gym, he had more success. In fact, this is what he ultimately found worked best because it reminded him of doing physical training in the military and it didn't interfere with spending time with his fiancée. He also found that when he went to the gym in the mornings, it tended to put him in a better frame of mind during his workday, so he was less likely to feel irritable or anxious on the days he went to the gym.

Experimenting with Days and Times

Karl noticed that he had more success at different days or times during the week. What have you noticed about days or times when you are more or less successful in taking steps toward your goal?

_____

_____

_____

_____

_____

Consider different approaches to meet the same goal. Annie very much wanted her girls to have time with friends and feel more independent. After realizing sending her daughter on a sleepover with people she didn't know felt overwhelming, she first encouraged her daughter to have a pizza and movie night at their house. She used this as an opportunity to talk more with the friend's parents. When they reciprocated with an invitation to take her daughters skating, Annie agreed and felt fairly comfortable. She then asked her sister, whom she felt was very safe, if the girls could have a sleepover at her house. This still felt like a stretch to Annie but a doable stretch in which her anxiety was offset by feeling good to be allowing her daughters these experiences.

Karl had always lifted free weights to build strength. However, he was aware that over the past ten years, his body was more prone to injury and worried that this might set him up for joint problems that could sideline his progress. So instead of planning to do free weights every time he went to the gym, he decided to intersperse his routine with some days dedicated to core strength, some to yoga, and some to calisthenics. This still helped him advance toward his weight-training goals, but the variety in exercises helped him reduce his risk for injury and kept him from falling into a "rut" because he liked the variety of workouts over the course of his week.

Trying Different Approaches

Now your turn—if you've tried an activity and found that it was too much too fast, what is another approach you could try that keeps you moving toward your ultimate goal?

_____

_____

_____

_____

Involve others to keep up your momentum. Karl had always lifted weights with a partner. However, he no longer had anyone in his life who he knew lifted weights. Karl took two different approaches to fix this problem. First, when he did go to the gym, he went at the same time each day (morning). Soon, he began to recognize other people in the gym. He looked for someone who seemed to be lifting at approximately the same level and began to ask another guy to "spot" him when he was trying to advance his weight targets. Over time, he became friendly with the other man and found that if he missed a day, his new "gym buddy" would ask him if everything was okay when he returned to the gym. Karl liked this sense of accountability. In addition, although Karl's fiancée had no interest in lifting weights, she did enjoy yoga classes. So twice a week, she would join Karl in his morning yoga class. Karl liked getting to know other guys at the gym and having his fiancée join him for yoga, because these things represented his "two-fors"(as in, two for the price of one)—he was making progress with his health and fitness goals while finally working to improve and expand his social life.

Bringing Others on Board

(available at http://www.newharbinger.com/43072)

Think about who else in your life you would like to have "on board" with your goals, in order to support you. Write their name(s) below.

_____

_____

_____

How could they be most helpful to you in your progress?

_____

_____

Write down your plan for who you will ask for help, how you'll go about it, and what you'll ask for, specifically.

_____

_____

_____

_____

Going Too Slowly

We have outlined some of the challenges around pacing that arise from overreaching in the initial action steps you take toward your recovery from PTSD. In our experience, this is the most common pacing challenge: taking action steps that are too big; becoming frustrated, stressed, or "triggered"; and then setting yourself up to return to TRAPs. However, sometimes, starting out too small or limiting yourself to making change in only one domain of your life can get in the way of gathering momentum.

Problems with Underreaching

As we did with overreaching, let's look at some ways that underreaching can be problematic.

PROBLEM 1: TAKING TOO SMALL OF A STEP

In line with her goal of "getting her life back," Annie was aware that she needed to get more comfortable in situations in which people are around and behind her, like at a store, in the elevator at work, or in the gym. She began by going to her neighborhood grocery store and choosing to go to the check-out line (where people could stand behind her) rather than the self-check-out. She initially felt some success but did not feel that her life was improving in any meaningful way and began to get discouraged, like she was "stuck in first gear."

At this point, it would be useful for Annie to take a bigger step, something that is a bit more of a challenge and gets her in contact with the life she wants to have. Given Annie's goals, examples could be (1) going shopping with a friend or her daughters (this would be in line with her goal of improving her relationships, while also helping her gain comfort with people in stores), (2) taking a yoga class and positioning herself in a different part of the room each time she went (in line with her goal of improving self-care), and (3) going for coffee with a coworker and sitting in the middle of the small café (again, toward her goal of improving relationships).

Reflecting on Underreaching Problem 1

Are there any ways that Annie's experience applies to you? Consider the action steps you've been taking so far toward your goals, and reflect on whether it might be time to challenge yourself a bit further. And, like with Annie, make sure your action steps are helping you experience the kind of life you want to have.

Goal: _____

Steps I've taken toward this goal: _____

_____

A bigger (or different) step I could take that would help me experience more of the life I am seeking: _

_____

_____

Goal: _____

Steps I've taken toward this goal: _____

_____

A bigger (or different) step I could take that would help me experience more of the life I am seeking: _

_____

_____

PROBLEM 2: ONLY FOCUSING ON ONE GOAL AT A TIME

With the effort that Karl put into resuming his weight lifting, he started to notice positive changes. He was feeling stronger and more confident and had a regular weight-lifting "buddy" at the gym. He was comfortable at the gym and began to feel that he was reclaiming this part of his life. However, other areas of his life felt stagnant. His fiancée often commented that he didn't seem "present" to her, even when they were alone together; he had to admit, he did often feel disengaged and distracted. Although Karl hated his job, he had stopped looking for other work and spent a fair amount of time at home, playing video games. While he had an interest in returning to church, he hadn't taken any steps to do so.

Can you relate to Karl's situation? Have you taken action toward one goal but neglected others? For some people, it takes so much effort to get started on one goal that it's hard to consider taking on more. And for some, early success in one area can then make that activity serve as a bit of avoidance to engaging in others! Karl was at risk for falling into that TRAP, as weight lifting started taking up more and more of his time and he would often choose an evening workout over a date night with his fiancée.

Annie also had difficulty attending to multiple goals at the same time. In her case, she felt so busy and stressed already, she didn't know how to find the time or energy to do anything more. Her daughters were her top priority, and she made sure she had time for them in the evenings and on weekends. She loved being a clinical social worker and working directly with clients, but she put in long hours and found the work emotionally taxing (particularly since her trauma). She knew she would feel better if she exercised more or could get to a yoga class, but she didn't know how to fit this in. She wished she had more friendships and support in her life, but this too felt daunting. When she considered how she could make progress in these other domains, she quickly became overwhelmed, wondering where she would find the time to do all these new activities (that also feel stressful) when she most often felt like she was "barely holding it together" with the day-to-day demands.

Reflecting on Underreaching Problem 2

Does Annie's predicament feel familiar? Take a moment to reflect on your multiple goals and competing demands and complete the following sentences.

I feel that most of my time and energy is spent _____

_____

_____ .

I wish I could find time and energy for _____

_____

_____ .

I've had difficulty attending to some of my goals because _____

_____

_____ .

Building Momentum

We have a few more suggestions on how to refine the pace and focus of your action steps, in this case, to build momentum and attend to multiple goals.

Look where you want to go. A guideline for driving safely on icy roads when you start to skid is to keep your focus on where you want to go; by doing so you self-correct and keep the car on the road. Similarly, to build momentum in your life, it is important to take steps that are out of your comfort zone (the icy road). If you have found that your steps are too small, then you'll really need to encourage yourself to take bigger challenges. This is more doable if you know the direction you are heading and can choose an activity that allows you to experience the benefit to your life. If the activity is fairly far removed from the ultimate goal (for example, you want to work on getting a different job but first you have to go to a store to buy new clothes), bring to mind the image of the goal you are working toward (for example, the job you'd like to have and how you'd like to feel in that job).

Spread out your time and energy so that you are pursuing multiple valued life goals, not just one or two. When choosing several goals to start, consider the ease of pursuing these goals, which ones will be the most rewarding, and which ones might make subsequent goals easier to attain (for example, first prioritizing health and sleep might make the goal of going back to school more attainable).

Karl decided to add in working on his relationship with his fiancée (since he cared about her deeply and didn't want to lose this relationship) and looking for a new job. He had awareness that he was still falling into avoidance patterns with both of these goals. He talked about this with his fiancée and together they made plans for more structured time together (going out at least one night a week, doing some type of outdoor activity together on the weekend, and having at least an hour together in the evenings at home). He was going to practice mindfulness during their time together to stay more engaged. He was also aware of having a fear of being vulnerable and set out to take some action steps by sharing more of his thoughts and feelings with his fiancée. Also, during some of their evenings at home, Karl talked with her about his steps toward looking for a new job. This helped him move forward on both his goal of finding a job as well as connecting more with his fiancée.

For Annie, trying to focus on more than one goal was complicated by having too many demands and not enough time. She used her Daily Activity and Mood Monitoring Chart to reexamine how she was spending her time each week and how these activities made her feel. She realized that she was setting aside most of her weekends and evenings for her daughters, yet they were getting to an age where they were wanting more time to themselves and with friends. Annie could support her daughters' growing independence by using some of her weekend time for other goals.

She began to set aside time two weeknights and on Saturday and Sunday mornings for exercise. Toward her goal of establishing more relationships, she used times that her daughters were engaged in other activities (with friends, at sports activities, at their dad's) to make walking and coffee dates with people at work and other parents whom she wanted to know better. Feeling more "fueled up" by these value- and goal-based activities improved her enjoyment of work and weekends and helped her feel like she was making progress in multiple areas of her life.

Don't forget to put energy into activities that bring you pleasure and rejuvenation (and not just the ones that are taxing or in the service of others). Living with PTSD can be exhausting. Your body and mind are frequently on hyper-alert and you likely find yourself reacting strongly to sights, sounds, smells, and events in your environment. If you have found yourself taking too small steps toward change, it's likely because of the toll you've experienced when you do engage. For this reason, it's important early on to pursue some goals and activities that quickly bring you good feelings and a sense of rejuvenation. As Annie discovered above, by spending some time pursuing goals that rejuvenated her (like exercise), she had more energy and motivation for her other goals. Also consider "mini-vacations" from pursuing goals at all; if you've been pushing yourself to engage in activities and are feeling the toll of this, give yourself breaks— like a day off to hike, binge watch TV, or sleep. The trick is to do this strategically and intentionally, with the goal of rejuvenation, being mindful that you don't fall back into TRAPS!

How Can I Build Momentum and Rejuvenate?

Think about how you might apply the above approaches to your life.

If you've only been pursuing one goal at a time, what could be some other goals you could pursue?

_____

_____

In line with your goals, can you choose an activity to pursue now that would give you a sense of pleasure and/or rejuvenation?

_____

_____

_____

If you were to have a "me day" in which the goal was to rest and rejuvenate, what would that look like?

_____

_____

_____

_____

_____

Summary

To maximize your gains with behavioral activation, consider your pace and breadth of change. Avoid taking on too much too fast, and use the strategies you've learned to gain momentum if you feel you're moving too slowly. In reality, most people vacillate between the two during the course of recovery and this is to be expected. Much like a driver on a road trip going across different terrain and experiencing a range of weather conditions, being skillful requires assessing what's needed in the moment and adjusting to the circumstances (sometimes slowing down, sometimes speeding up, taking the curves with care, and sometimes rolling the windows down and driving with abandon).

Keep your mechanic mind active, staying curious about any challenges you encounter. While you've worked hard with observations about Karl, Annie, and your own life and made some decisions about possible alternatives, we know change is hard and sometimes takes concerted effort to dig in and troubleshoot. Good mechanics know that their initial diagnosis of a problem isn't always the right one, and they need to consider other reasons for automobile troubles.

In the next chapter we will give you additional tools for your mechanic mind as we review more specific problem-solving strategies. Some of these may be new skills, whereas others may serve as useful reminders for approaches you already know. Remember that these pacing (and problem-solving) skills will serve you well, both in the beginning of behavioral activation and throughout your recovery.

CHAPTER 7

Applying Problem-Solving Strategies to Overcome Barriers to Activation

The behavioral activation approach to overcoming PTSD is centered on identifying your avoidance patterns (TRAPs) and developing alternative coping strategies to get you back on TRAC to living a meaningful life. However, sometimes there are other practical barriers to activation that don't directly relate to PTSD avoidance. Going back to our driving metaphor, these practical barriers can be represented by heavy traffic or road construction; you have a path you are motivated to follow, but factors outside of your control are preventing you from making progress.

For example, if you have a goal of increasing your physical fitness by swimming regularly, but you don't have a car available to you to drive to a nearby swimming pool, *lack of transportation* can represent a barrier to meeting your activation goals. Physical constraints, time constraints, limited finances, limited nearby availability for pursuing desired activities, transportation challenges, and geographical challenges (e.g., winter conditions) all represent practical barriers to activation. In this chapter, we will present some key principles of problem solving and examples of how to use them to overcome practical barriers to meeting your activation goals. Take a moment to read about some of Karl's challenges meeting his activation goals related to spirituality.

Karl had been raised Catholic but drifted away from the church in his young adulthood and no longer felt that this specific faith represented his spiritual life. He had attended several services at the local Episcopalian church and found that it was possibly a "good fit"; however, his fiancée wasn't particularly religious or interested in attending church and, because of her work schedule, Sundays were one of the few days of the week that they could spend together alone. Both Karl's relationship and his faith were important values, but his schedule made it difficult to attend the Episcopalian services without sacrificing time with his fiancée. As he weighed his options, Karl became frustrated and depressed. He was trying so hard to climb out of the ruts that PTSD had caused in his life and meeting up against this roadblock felt discouraging.

Can you relate to these types of challenges facing Karl? Have you encountered situations where, because of time constraints, you haven't been able to pursue a valued activity or make progress on an activation goal? Have these sorts of roadblocks caused you to lose momentum or hope?

Anticipate Practical Barriers

When we develop plans or strategies for change, we often begin by imagining what we want as the outcome and visualizing the positive results that would come from making changes. It's like planning a cross-country road trip; you imagine speeding along the open highway, the sun shining, and seeing beautiful scenery along the way. Imagining the results is often an important motivator and can be useful as a behavioral activation strategy to develop action steps. However, when we encounter a practical barrier to taking action steps toward our goals—in the case of our road trip, a car breakdown, traffic jams, or rainy road conditions—it is easy to become frustrated and discouraged.

So an important first step in problem solving around practical barriers is to recognize that these types of challenges will likely arise somewhere along the road. It may be helpful to anticipate some of the challenges you might encounter before you begin to take action steps so you are prepared (both practically and emotionally) for encountering barriers.

Take a moment to think about your current and most important behavioral activation goals and planned action steps; what types of practical barriers might arise as you prepare and take steps toward these new behavior targets? We provide an example below to help you get started.

Value and/or Goal: Improve my health

Action Step: Join a gym and start work-out routine

Potential Practical Barriers:

1. Cost (too expensive)?

2. Distance to travel—too far out of my way to be convenient?

3. *Not open during the hours I would want to go?*

4. *Crowds/wait times—too many people using the machines?*

5. *Not owning the proper work-out clothes?*

Identifying Practical Barriers to My Behavioral Activation

(available at http://www.newharbinger.com/43072)

Now it's your turn. Consider three of your value or goals, action steps, and the potential barriers to taking those steps.

Value and/or Goal: _____

Action-Step: _____

Potential Practical Barriers:

1. _____

2. _____

3. _____

4. _____

5. _____

Value and/or Goal: _____

Action-Step: _____

Potential Practical Barriers:

1. _____

2. _____

3. _____

4. _____

5. _____

Value and/or Goal: _____

Action-Step: _____

Potential Practical Barriers:

1. _____

2. _____

3. _____

4. _____

5. _____

Brainstorm

An important first step to effective problem solving is brainstorming solutions. Brainstorming means developing *multiple ideas, without censoring anything,* for how you might overcome or go around barriers and still achieve your goals. For example, let's return to the idea of a cross-country road tip. Your first plan is to travel by driving your car. But what if your car were to break down? You could brainstorm all the ways to get it fixed (try it yourself, take it to the mechanic, ask a friend who is good with cars) or find another car (rent one, borrow a friend's, steal one—we're not censoring anything yet!). You could also brainstorm other ways of reaching your goal of a cross-country trip. You could take a bus, take a train, take an airplane ride, or even walk. In fact, to be really open to all possibilities, you could also take a boat (although not likely the fastest option!). Although you might not want to choose some or all these other options, you can recognize that there are multiple ways for you to overcome your barrier and reach your goal. Each of these might come with a different set of challenges. But knowing that you have other options can help you stay open to alternative approaches and avoid falling into some of the TRAPs that come with feelings of frustration or anxiety. In sum, it is important to be creative when you brainstorm, trying to always think "outside the box."

Brainstorming Practice

This exercise is meant to be a fun way to practice problem solving. Imagine you are trying to move your car (which is parked in the driveway) but can't get the engine to start. Make a list of all the alternative ways you might accomplish this goal. Don't worry about things being impractical (e.g., hiring a helicopter to lift the car from the driveway); just let your mind generate ideas as quickly and thoroughly as you can.

I could move my car without turning on the engine in the following ways:

1. _____

2. _____

3. _____

4. _____

5. _____

6. _____

7. _____

8. _____

9. _____

10. _____

The next step in brainstorming is to cross off the options that truly aren't possible, and circle the ones that have any possibility of working. Then start with the one that has the most likelihood of success first. If it doesn't work, then try the next. Try to stay flexible and open to the awareness that there are almost always more options to try.

Prepare for Challenges Through Proactive Planning

If you are planning a cross-country road trip, listing out the potential challenges you might encounter gives you some time to think about how you might handle each type of challenge. If you encounter a traffic jam, you might want to know what alternative routes exist, or account for the possible delay when planning your itinerary. You also might bring some of your favorite music or an audiobook to listen to if you are delayed. You might pack a cooler with drinks and snacks so that if your delay interferes with a mealtime stop, you aren't thirsty or hungry while you wait for the traffic to clear. Below is Karl's list of anticipated or potential practical barriers to his goals around spirituality, as well as some possible ways he might address these challenges.

Value and/or Goal: Spirituality: I want to find a way to weave my faith back into my life...I want to find a community of people who share my values.

Action Steps:

I will look up the times/dates of Episcopalian services; I will talk to my fiancée about my desire to reconnect with my spiritual side and find a way to have that represented in my life; I will explore other ways (other than church services) to represent my faith and connect with a like-minded community.

Potential Practical Barriers:

1. Maybe the only times I can go to services are when I could spend time with my fiancée.

2. Maybe I won't actually feel at home in the community, even after I try going regularly.

3. Maybe talking about this challenge will hurt my fiancée's feelings and make her feel as though I don't prioritize her.

4. Maybe I'll be too tired and worn out from the week of work to feel like going to church on Sundays.

5. If I do attend services, maybe I will get triggered by the crowds and people I don't know.

Things I can do to prepare for these potential barriers:

1. I can go on the church website and investigate the times of the services, as well as other ways to participate in the community (e.g., prayer meetings, volunteering, or meeting with other church members outside of church services).

2. If I don't feel like this is a good fit for me over time, I can explore other church services. Maybe there will be different churches and communities that will ultimately be a better fit. I'll make a list of other possible churches to visit if this one doesn't work out.

3. I can talk to my fiancée about my worries and fears. She has been very supportive of the types of changes I am trying to make in my life. Maybe if I explain that this fits into my recovery plan, she might not be hurt (and might even support me). I can also let her know that I'm looking at other ways to explore andparticipate in the church—ways that wouldn't interfere with our time together.

4. If I want to prioritize pursuing my faith and participation in churchon Sundays (or other days of the week), I can adjust my schedule the day prior so that I plan to do less, spend some time "resting" and give myself the best possible chance of feeling energized and focused for when I do try attending the services.

5. I can start out sitting in the back of the church. I might also explore which service (the early service or the latter service) has fewer people in attendance. I can always get up and "take a breather" if I feel overwhelmed.

Preparing for Potential Barriers

(available at http://www.newharbinger.com/43072)

Now we want to ask you to brainstorm some ways that you might address and overcome the practical barriers you listed above regarding one of your top three behavioral activation goals. (We encourage you to go through this process for your other identified goals as well.) Again, don't overthink these; just list what comes to mind and try and generate as many possible ways to overcome or address these challenges as you can. Remember to think outside the box when generating problem-solving strategies. Then, take a moment to notice any PTSD-related triggered response or avoidance patterns (TRAPs) that might arise should you try to apply these to solve the practical barriers in front of you. For example, if you notice yourself becoming nervous about addressing travel barriers (e.g., taking a bus to the gym), take note of the possibility that PTSD-related avoidance might be present (e.g., "Ever since my military service, being in crowds make me feel unsafe" or, "I get panicky when I'm not in control of the vehicle because of my accident").

Things I can do to prepare for potential barriers to action steps:

1. _____

2. _____

3. _____

4. _____

5. _____

PTSD TRAPs that might arise:

1. _____

2. _____

3. _____

4. _____

5. _____

Remain Curious and Flexible in Your Problem Solving

It is important when problem solving around practical barriers that you practice adopting a mechanic's mindset of curiosity ("Let's see if I can find another way of doing this!") and remain flexible in your efforts to generate solutions. For example, if you plan for a cross-country road trip, you might think ahead to imagine all sorts of potential roadblocks. However, you may likely still come upon some barriers that you hadn't anticipated. Or even if you encounter an anticipated challenge, you might find that your planned solution doesn't work, or works but isn't the best way to help you get back on the road quickly. For this reason, we encourage you to practice having a "curious mindset" (or mechanics mind) when evaluating what works and doesn't work to overcome barriers.

Take a moment to read about Karl's first experiences problem solving around practical barriers, his "lessons learned" attitude, and the ways he tried to cultivate an open, creative process in developing new problem-solving approaches.

Karl had a goal of improving his physical conditioning through weight lifting. He had encountered some PTSD-related TRAPs (e.g., busy gym hours would trigger his feeling of being "on guard") and found alternative ways of coping (e.g., going to the gym during "off hours," practicing mindfulness during his weight lifting, and listening to a relaxing music list he had made to help him feel calmer). However, he found that his left shoulder simply wouldn't bear the weight of the barbells he used for shoulder exercises, and his back injuries prevented him from progressing in the other upper-body strength training he had always done before his deployment.

Karl developed a problem-solving plan of using resistance bands rather than weights so he could have more control over the impact on his shoulder and back. Although this worked better than the free weights he was used to using, it didn't really feel as satisfying and he felt limited to the degree he could advance his strength goals. So Karl set out to develop a wider range of possible alternatives and made the following list (without spending too much time considering each possible solution):

1. Go to a physical therapist and ask for exercises to address and improve my shoulder and back pain

2. Set up an appointment with a personal trainer to see if there are other weight-lifting exercises I could try to target my upper body

3. Start to swim to develop shoulder and back strength

4. Try a "power yoga" class

5. Try using a rowing machine

6. Research and try body-weight resistance training exercises

7. Talk to a primary care provider about supplements or nonaddictive pain medications to help me manage pain and discomfort (assuming the physical therapist approved my exercises)

Although Karl did experience some frustration and disappointment with his first attempts to resume weight training, he worked hard to stay curious about finding other ways to accomplish his goal while working around his shoulder and back injuries. He repeated a phrase he had learned in the military—"Adapt and overcome!"—whenever he found himself feeling discouraged.

Use Your Social Support Network to Help Develop Solutions

In chapter 9, we will further discuss benefits of using your social support people (e.g., family, friends, coworkers) to help you take action steps and meet and maintain your behavioral activation goals. However, we want to also encourage you to use people close to you to help problem solve around some of the practical barriers you might encounter. For example, if transportation barriers arise, you might ask yourself, *Are there people who might be able to help me get to where I need to go? Would they help me out occasionally or could I rely on them regularly?* The people close to you might help you directly to overcome practical barriers, or they might help you generate some ideas for how you could problem solve around concrete challenges you encounter. Can you imagine calling a family member or friend and asking for their help generating solutions? This type of support can be very helpful for building support over time and helping you stay open and creative to finding ways to overcome practical barriers.

Here is an example of how Annie used her social support network to help her overcome some practical barriers to her action steps:

Annie was taking action to improve her quality of life, both at work and at home. She recognized that she tended to overwork (she had identified this as a TRAP) and fill her nonwork hours with caring for her two girls. She had recently made some positive steps toward increasing her time with her work friend and her sister, and relied on a close friend to help her with child care so she could feel that she was keeping her children safe and well cared for while she was out. However, she was struggling to find time solely dedicated for herself. It seemed there simply weren't enough hours in the day to spend doing some "self-care" after she tried to meet the demands at work, the responsibilities of her children, and fostering new friendships. She decided to make a list of people she could approach, for both help and advice. She felt that her immediate supervisor at work could understand her challenges, as she was also a single parent with significant work-related responsibilities. She also knew she could ask her close friend for some help brainstorming solutions.

Annie was pleasantly surprised when she approached her supervisor to ask for help carving out some personal time; her supervisor recognized Annie's "workaholic" tendencies, and although she relied on Annie's dedication to the hospital, she also didn't want to have a valued employee burn out. Annie and her supervisor sat down and made a list of her work duties and helped prioritize them, in terms of both the hospital's needs and Annie's preferences. They then developed a plan to delegate some of Annie's tasks to other social work employees so that Annie could leave on time most days of the week. This created a ninety-minute window for Annie to exercise, read, or simply relax before the girls needed to be picked up from their afterschool activities. Annie also talked to her close friend who had found some creative ways to carve out "me-time" in her day, including listening to books on tape during her commute to work, getting up early in the morning for brief meditation sessions, and creating reading time with her girls, where they read books separately while hanging out on the couch. None of these had occurred to Annie, and she felt grateful she had such a helpful and creative friend!

My Support People

(available at http://www.newharbinger.com/43072)

Now take a moment and make two lists: one of people you might ask for direct help, and the other of people you might ask for advice or help problem solving around challenges.

People I can ask for practical help (e.g., travel, child care):

1. _____

2. _____

3. _____

4. _____

5. _____

People I can ask for advice or to help me generate possible solutions:

1. _____

2. _____

3. _____

4. _____

5. _____

A comment about trust: Take a moment to notice if you found yourself reluctant to ask for help from others. For people with PTSD, "opening up" and trusting others can sometimes be very difficult. You might also have difficulty letting others know you would like help, perhaps believing you should be able to do this on your own. There might be some PTSD-related TRAPs buried in this exercise specific to trust and reliance on others. We will dedicate more discussion to this topic in chapter 9, but for now, we encourage you to apply the TRAC strategies you learned in chapter 5 to try and develop alternative ways for you to ask for advice and help.

Find Alternative Goals and Action Steps to Increase Happiness

Previously, we mentioned that there might be multiple ways for you to meet your behavioral activation goals. We want to encourage you to use the skills we have outlined to explore these options, including planning ahead and identifying practical barriers, brainstorming various ways to overcome practical barriers, seeking out support and advice from others, and adopting a "curious mind" (mechanics mind) perspective so that you can learn from challenges and adjust accordingly. However, we also want to encourage you to stay open to the possibility that you might in fact need or want to change your goals along the way. When considering resetting or adapting your behavioral activation goals, it is very useful to stay aware of the original values that drove you to make the initial goals. It may also be helpful to analyze why certain goals appealed to you in the first place.

Some of Karl's problem-solving strategies represent this approach; although Karl had originally set out to return to weight lifting, his injuries were practical barriers to doing so. His brainstorming efforts included different ways he might return to weight lifting (e.g., seeking out advice from a physical trainer), while others addressed a different path toward improving his fitness (e.g., swimming). Both of these avenues reflected actions he could take to help him move forward with his value of physical fitness and health. Karl also found it was helpful to dive into the "why" behind his values of fitness and health in order to develop other potential goals that represented this value. Read Karl's experience of reassessing his weight-lifting goals specific to his values around health and fitness routines.

Karl continued to feel significant pain when he tried to resume weight lifting; a visit to a physical therapist yielded some important new exercises that he could use to help his injury, but he was told that he would likely never be able to safely free-lift weights without significant risk of further injury. He had tried to stay open to other ways to pursue fitness, including swimming and yoga classes. They certainly helped him feel healthier. But he found that neither activity produced the same sense of satisfaction. So he decided to break down what he had liked so much about lifting weights.

First, he liked the personal challenge of increasing the weight that he could lift. Neither swimming nor yoga had this kind of "self-test" aspect to the activity. He also enjoyed the banter he used to have with other people in the weight room. He had developed many good friends through weight lifting, and the activity had a social quality that neither swimming nor yoga provided. Finally, lifting weights had helped Karl's confidence in terms of his ability to protect himself and the people he loved. With shoulder injuries and a bad back, he felt less confident in his ability to defend himself.

Karl thought about other types of activities that shared some of the same components of weight lifting. Before the military, Karl had not grown up around firearms or spent time target shooting or hunting. However, he had come to enjoy this part of his training. Because parts of Karl's traumas involved witnessing and causing injury and death, he knew he wouldn't enjoy hunting. However, he wondered if target shooting would be a different type of activity that could allow him to test himself. Because he had some military friends who lived in the area, he thought he could probably find others who might want to join him at the shooting range; Karl noted that this would be another one of his "two-fors," representing both an action step toward his goal of improving his social and relationship network as well as a way for him act on his values of self-challenge. Finally, Karl felt that working to maintain his proficiency with firearms was another way for him to feel safe and ready to defend himself if needed.

My Alternative Goals and Action Steps

Review your earlier list of goals, possible practical barriers, and problem-solving strategies. If you were to encounter significant challenges to overcoming any of the practical barriers you listed, are there other types of activities that might share common features with your behavioral activation goals? Take a moment to explore alternative goals that might also help to improve your satisfaction with life.

Original goal(s):

_____

_____

_____

Aspects of the goal that are most appealing:

_____

_____

_____

_____

Other goals or activities that share some of the aspects you listed above:

_____

_____

_____

_____

_____

Summary

In this chapter, we introduced the idea of problem solving around practical barriers that are interfering with your progress toward achieving your behavioral activation goals. Practical barriers are similar to TRAPs but may exist regardless of any sort of PTSD-related avoidance. By anticipating practical barriers and planning ahead, you will be better prepared to overcome challenges that might arise. Remember to brainstorm multiple solutions and to remain curious about the process of trial-and-error, recognizing that the lessons learned will serve you in the future. Relying on social support people, both for practical assistance and help brainstorming, will greatly increase the chances that you overcome practical barriers. Finally, remain open to finding other types of goals and activities that might be different in form but share important features with your original behavioral activation goals.

In the next chapter we will discuss ways to pay attention to your experience in the present moment as you activate toward recovery. Sometimes referred to as "mindfulness," this attention to experience skill will help you get the most out of your activation efforts. It will also help you avoid unwittingly falling into TRAPs along the way.

CHAPTER 8

Employing Mindfulness to Maximize Your Activation

We are all guilty of losing track of our attention at times. In fact, one of the ways that we are able to function effectively in the world is our ability to cruise along on autopilot while we do simple tasks such as wash the dishes, fold laundry, or even walk down the street. If we had to put our full focus on each aspect of these activities (*now I put the plate in the water, now I move the scrub brush across the surface of the plate, now I rinse the plate in clean water*), our ability to get things done would be significantly impaired!

However, there can be significant costs to functioning on autopilot; when we lose our focus on the immediate moment, our mind can take us in very different directions and we can lose the opportunity to "record" a particular experience. In this chapter, we will introduce the skill of paying attention to your experiences *while* you are having them. You may find that some of these experiences aren't as terrific as you had hoped, while others might exceed your expectations. By learning to pay attention in the moment, you will be better positioned to evaluate your progress toward recovery and reap some of the rewards that you have worked so hard to achieve.

Attention to Experience

Let's say you set off for your grand cross-country road trip, but as you pull out of your hometown, you begin to worry that you forgot something important for your trip. You go over and over things that you have packed and your list of necessary items. Finally, you are reassured that you have all the important items packed, so you turn on the special music you had recorded for your first leg of the journey.

However, you become anxious about the heavy traffic and begin to worry that you have underestimated the travel time to your planned destination for the night. Suddenly, you begin to worry that your entire itinerary will be thrown off. You begin to think back to other trips you have taken where things didn't go according to plan and start to ruminate about all the reasons why you struggled to enjoy your travel. As the hours of driving pass, you spend so much time in your head that you suddenly realize you have not paid attention to the scenery or the music soundtrack you had made for the road. You have missed the very thing you had set out to experience!

Does any of this sound familiar to you? Welcome to the challenges of being human. We are gifted the amazing abilities to think backward in time and to imagine the future. These are generally helpful abilities that allow us to learn from the past and plan ahead for our future. However, many of us find that these patterns of *rumination* (thinking repeatedly about the same past events) or *worry* (anxiously imagining all the potential challenges we might encounter in life) interfere with our ability to stay present in the moment. And because we stop paying attention to our experience, we lose the ability to benefit or learn from what is directly in front of us.

Further, research studies have found that people with PTSD may experience attentional difficulties, as they are both more likely to notice or perceive threat cues *and* evidence greater avoidance of threat cues in their environment (e.g., Iacoviello et al. 2014); this type of interference in your attention and focus could greatly impact your experience of activities out in the world. Because of these patterns of attention toward and away from threat cues, you may need to put effort into focusing on all the aspects of your daily activities in order to gain a full appreciation of the benefits of value-based activities.

We have asked you to put in a great deal of effort to evaluate your personal values, set behavioral activation goals, and take action steps toward these goals. Wouldn't it be a shame for you to be doing all these things and find that you are missing out on the experiences you've invested so much time and effort into having? It would be akin to driving past all of the sightseeing destinations you researched for your road trip but never getting out of your car to actually see them!

A first step toward increasing your attention to experience is to increase your awareness of your mind's tendencies to drift away from the present and toward other things, including past events (like trauma memories), future concerns (for example, fears or worry about safety threats), or selective features of the present (such as fear cues). To gain a better sense of where you mind tends to take you outside of the present moment, we want to invite you to complete the following exercise.

My Wandering Mind

(available at http://www.newharbinger.com/43072)

Sit down in a relatively quiet, comfortable space. Have a pen and paper nearby and set a timer for five or ten minutes. If you're comfortable doing so, close your eyes. During this time let you mind wander wherever it might take you and make simple notes to record all of the different thought content, as well as any emotional reactions you might have to the content of your thoughts (you can pause your timer while you write). Try not to "control" your thoughts or direct them toward any particular topic. Simply observe and follow your thought sequences and make brief notes to help you observe the ways your mind wanders.

Thought	Emotion(s) Attached to Thought

What did you notice? Were there any patterns to the thoughts and how they related to one another? Did you find any strong emotions attached to any particular thought(s)? Did your PTSD "show up" in any of your thoughts or emotions during the exercise? Can you recognize the costs of these thought wanderings regarding your efforts to activate toward recovery?

Take a moment to read about Karl's first efforts to attend to his experiences and his struggles.

One of Karl's most profound lessons from his time in a war zone related to an appreciation for "the small things." During his deployment, he realized how much he had taken for granted the daily comforts of life back home, such as air conditioning, clean clothes, and freshly made food. Karl also found that, although combat was at times incredibly intense, it also seemed simpler—he only had to focus on the immediate tasks at hand and didn't spend time worrying about other daily stressors such as traffic, bills, or yardwork. He swore to himself that, after he returned from his deployment, he would maintain this appreciation for the simple pleasures in life and not "sweat the small stuff." However, he quickly found that the stress of adjusting to civilian life made it difficult to keep this simple life mindset and appreciation for daily pleasures.

Now that he was working on behavioral activation and trying to include new activities in his daily routines, Karl noticed that he was often distracted. When out in public, he tended to still scan his environment for safety threats, leaving him distracted from what he was doing (when taking action steps toward recovery). Sometimes a smell or noise could bring up strong memories of his deployment, and he would find himself "lost" in a memory. At other times he found himself playing out different scenarios and making "action plans" in his head, planning for possible attacks. He initially found that, while he would meet his behavioral activation goals for the week, he often couldn't really notice or remember how it felt at the time to accomplish these goals. Instead, he noticed feeling keyed up and stressed.

Attention to experience involves purposely shifting your focus to the activity in which you are engaging and your associated experiences with this activity. This includes paying attention to any of your sensory experiences (what you see, hear, touch, smell, or taste) as well as your thoughts and emotions in reaction to your experience. Attention to experience also involves noticing when your attention is *not* focused on your present experience, and gently pulling it back to your experience.

Let's say you've planned a dinner out with your partner. You're looking forward to spending time with this person and you've picked a restaurant you've been wanting to try. When you get there you notice feeling keyed up. When you sit down you find yourself scanning the room, checking out the other patrons and looking for the exits. What could you shift your focus to instead, to engage more in your experience of having dinner out with your partner? Options include noticing what your partner looks like in this moment, paying attention to what they are saying, noticing the smells in the room, really tasting your food, and when you get distracted by scanning or remembering, noticing the distraction and gently pulling your attention back to your partner and your meal.

Here's how Karl worked on building attention to experience.

Karl started putting an effort into paying closer attention to what he was doing, when he was doing it. Before he began any new activity, he would stop for a moment and focus his attention back to the moment. It sometimes took a lot of effort to stay focused on the present moment and avoid scanning his environment for threats. In fact, he often found that he would quickly become distracted again by his patterns of vigilance but told himself that each time he noticed that his mind had wandered back toward scanning his environment, he simply would gently bring it back into the moment. Sometimes he would become frustrated with himself, but he would remind himself that this was a new skill and that he would need to practice it before it became more familiar.

Building My Attention to Experience

(available at http://www.newharbinger.com/43072)

Consider ways you might be able to increase your attention to experience of an activity you are working to increase. Pick an activity that you would like to try, or something you have already tried but did not enjoy as much (or get as much out of) as you thought you would. In the space below, identify what you could attend to and what might be (or were) your distractions (not all categories will apply in all situations!):

Activity: _____

What I could focus my eyes on:

_____

What I could listen to/for:

_____

What I could smell:

_____

What I could feel with my touch:

_____

What I could taste:

_____

What I could pay attention to in my body:

_____

Where might my attention get pulled to instead? (Consider sights, thoughts, emotions, etc.):

_____

If my attention gets pulled away from my present experience, what could I refocus on?

_____

While this may seem like an easy enough concept to grasp, it is frequently difficult to maintain this kind of focus. In particular, you might find that the content of your thoughts is associated with some strong emotions. That may be especially true if you become triggered by something in your environment, causing you to revisit thoughts and emotions connected to your traumatic event(s). Furthermore, once your PTSD becomes triggered it may be difficult to separate yourself from powerful emotions such as fear, anger, or grief. Strong emotions will lead to more thoughts, which can lead to more emotions.

In the same way that hitting black ice while driving can prompt you to hit the brakes, your instinct to stop these difficult emotions can be powerful. However, slamming on the breaks while you are sliding on black ice will often lead you to lose control over your vehicle and actually cause the types of accident you are trying to avoid. Similarly, trying to suppress powerful emotions can cause you to spin out of control and lose control over your thoughts and emotions. Rather than trying to overcontrol these thoughts or feelings or swerve out of the way, we encourage you to practice "coasting through" these moments of powerful emotion while focusing your attention on where you want it to be (keep your eyes on the road).

Mindfulness

Attention to experience is similar to the concept and practice of *mindfulness*. Mindfulness has been defined as "paying attention in a particular way: on purpose, in the present moment, and nonjudgmentally" (Kabat-Zinn 1994, 4). So any practice that enhances mindfulness (e.g., meditation, yoga, martial arts) can help strengthen your ability to attend to your present experience.

Importantly, mindfulness can also help you notice when your PTSD becomes triggered and you have strong urges to escape and avoid (as described above). Notice that a key element of mindfulness is adopting a *nonjudgmental* perspective. This means letting go of *evaluations* of your thoughts or emotions as "good" or "bad" and instead simply noticing their *presence* and any associated urges in response to these thoughts and emotions. This too is often easier said than done, but there are a number of reasons why mindfulness can be a very helpful skill to cultivate for people with PTSD working on recovery.

First, a nonjudgmental stance toward your thoughts and emotional experiences can help you stay focused on the bigger picture and avoid falling back into TRAPs. For example, let's say you are working toward an action step related to increasing your social connections by spending time with close friends. If one of your friends happens to mention a movie that depicts a character with PTSD, you might become somewhat triggered and experience an impulse to withdraw from the situation (maybe making up an excuse for why you need to leave). Attending to your experience in a mindful, curious, and nonjudgmental way might allow you to simply notice the impulse to withdraw while also leaving you some room to instead make a decision to employ a TRAC coping strategy. You might say to yourself, *Oh isn't that interesting…I'm spending time with someone I care about and yet, when they mention something to do with PTSD, my avoidance symptoms suddenly prompt my brain to seek an escape…I wonder if letting them know that I just had a reaction to that topic might help me stay present and perhaps even deepen my connection with them.*

Second, a mindfulness perspective invites you back to each moment without an expectation that whatever you were thinking or feeling will be present again now or in the future. This is important because, if we simply observe our thoughts and feelings, we will notice that they tend to change very quickly; whereas if we "grab the wheel" and try and control them, they tend to stick around longer and have more of an impact. By keeping ourselves grounded in the moment, we can learn to trust that any PTSD triggered response will come and go on its own, without us needing to swerve to avoid it or grapple with it for hours at a time. Indeed, if you can coast through some difficult moments (icy patches) on the road to recovery, you'll find that you will regain control without having to take drastic actions.

A third reason why mindfulness is helpful to people with PTSD is that people with PTSD tend to "gloss over" nontrauma-related memories in their lives, including happy memories, such that people exposed to trauma have more difficulty recalling specifics related to their positive life experiences (Ono, Devilly, and Shum 2016). Because mindfulness encourages you to pay attention to the details of your experience, this deliberate attention to positive experiences may help you better encode these moments and later recall the details of your positive experiences.

So we have outlined reasons why paying attention to experiences is important for behavioral activation and the specific benefits of adopting a mindful, nonjudgmental way of observing your thoughts and emotions. But cultivating mindfulness is a skill that takes practice. As with anything, the more you practice mindfulness, the easier and more automatic it will become over time. Here are some common mindfulness exercises you can practice to help cultivate your ability to be mindfully present and aware in your day-to-day life.

Notice your breath. Paying attention to your breathing is a good way to focus on the present moment. For example, set a timer for five minutes and sit in a quiet space. Practice paying attention to the physical sensations of slowly inhaling and exhaling as you breathe (you could pay attention to the rise and fall of your stomach and chest or the sensations of the air going in and out of your nose). When your mind drifts to thoughts, emotions, or other distractions, you can note their presence (in a nonjudgmental, curious way, for example, *A thought about the conversation I had with my husband earlier today just came up*) and refocus back to your breath.

Practice mindful walking. Take a ten minute walk (preferably outside). Pay attention to the physical sensations you experience while lifting and placing each foot. If you are walking outside, notice things such as the air temperature, any natural landscape or vegetation you are walking past, sounds, or other things in your environment such as cars, houses, other people, or animals. Notice where you mind "lands" while walking. Without trying to do anything about your thoughts, stay curious and observe what types of thoughts or emotions arise. Notice how quickly they change (and or circle back) to different topics.

Eat in a mindful way. Choose something you enjoy eating and pay close attention to the experience of smelling, tasting, chewing, and swallowing the food as you eat. Notice the specific flavors that register while you eat. Notice any memories or other associations that might arise while eating this food.

Listen to a favorite piece of music. Pick a favorite song or musical piece and listen to it carefully, attending to the different instruments or voices that you hear. Notice the lyrics and any ways that they influence your thoughts or emotions as you listen. While listening, take note of other sights and sounds in your environment.

Take a warm bath or shower. Notice the sensation of the water on your skin. Pay attention to the sensation of your body coming into contact with the bathtub or shower stall. As you use soap or shampoo, register the smells and texture of the suds as you lather. Observe what types of thoughts or emotions arise and gently return your focus to the water on your skin.

Develop your own mindfulness exercise. You will notice some similarities while reviewing each of these suggested mindfulness exercises. Each exercise involves a simple task that does not require extensive planning, organizing, or effort to maintain. Each exercise has some aspect of repetition or point of focus for your mind to come back to in order to return to the present moment. Take a moment to consider some other activities like this, perhaps things that you already do, that you could use to practice mindfulness.

We encourage you to experiment with these suggested mindfulness exercises or develop your own. Notice which seem to come more easily to you or help you find a present-moment, nonjudgmental perspective. Perhaps you might try different exercises at different times during your day to see which work best and when.

Putting Mindfulness into Daily Practice

Some people dedicate hours each day to fostering mindfulness. We certainly support your doing as much practice as you can to develop this skill, but we also recognize that finding that sort of time and space in your day can be challenging. We think it is more important for you to adopt a daily ritual than to set aside a lengthy period of time to practice mindfulness. Thus, we suggest that you set aside a minimum of five minutes in the morning and five minutes in the evening to practice fostering a mindful perspective, learning to observe the internal and external experiences that are occurring each moment, and learning to watch your thoughts and emotions in a nonjudgmental, curious way.

It can also be helpful to remind yourself to come back to a mindfulness perspective during the day as you engage in daily activities or take action steps toward your recovery. Remembering to return to this perspective can be difficult, however. Some people we have worked with have found that scheduling reminders on their smartphone throughout the day is a useful prompt to take some time to come back to the present moment. Others have found that certain daily activities can be good reminders to practice mindfulness (for example, using each mealtime to practice mindful eating or practicing mindfulness each morning in the shower).

Mindfulness Worksheet

(available at http://www.newharbinger.com/43072)

Complete the following worksheet to help you schedule mindfulness practice into your day and apply the skill while you activate toward recovery.

Things I can do during the day to practice mindfulness:

(Circle all those that you think might work for you and/or create your own mindfulness rituals.)

Eat mindfully   Walk mindfully   Shower/bathe mindfully

Set phone reminders   Practice mindfulness at red lights

Practice mindfulness for three minutes before turning on the TV/computer/radio

My own daily mindfulness ritual(s):

1. _____

2. _____

3. _____

I will choose to practice _____ (specific activity from above) to foster mindfulness for a minimum of five minutes each morning. I'll schedule this practice for _____ a.m.

I will choose to practice _____ to foster mindfulness for a minimum of five minutes each evening. I'll schedule this practice for _____ p.m.

Now take a moment to read about Annie's use of mindfulness as a tool for maximizing her behavioral activation toward recovery for PTSD.

Annie began each morning by sitting quietly and focusing on her breathing. Right away, she became much more aware of the frequency of fear or threat-related thoughts she had each day. At first she felt embarrassed by this observation ("Jeez, my mind is like Chicken Little—the sky is always falling!"). However, she also tried to refrain from harsh self-judgment, and over the first couple of weeks, she began to feel some self-compassion ("Wow, no wonder I have struggled with concentration so much—my mind is constantly on red alert!").

Annie also noticed that by sitting quietly each morning and again each evening for five minutes to observe her breathing, she came to really appreciate this "space" in her day. Although she didn't try to set any agenda, she found that her mind would race ahead each morning, trying to "get ahead of the curve" of the day. As she practiced redirecting her thoughts back to the sensations she felt while breathing, she noticed that doing so would slightly lower her stress. It turned out to be a nice way to slow down before her day forced her to speed up. Likewise, her mind would often retrace her day during her evening mindfulness practice. However, by focusing on her breathing, she found that she could slow this down and find her way back to the (often pleasant) feeling of being tired and ready for bed.

Annie also decided that before she transitioned to a new activity, she would take a few moments to ground herself back into the moment, simply taking note of where her thoughts and emotions were. After doing this daily practice for several weeks, she found that she developed a greater ability to stay present when she was engaged in a high-value activity such as spending time her friend or daughters. Further, these activities were more enjoyable because she was really "taking it in" while they were occurring. This greater attention to the "bright spots" in her days and weeks also shifted Annie's overall sense of her life. She began to appreciate that a lot of things were going well for her and that, although she still had frequent moments of PTSD triggered responses, these moments occurred amid other moments of happiness and love. It wasn't as though her PTSD had disappeared; it was more like the rest of her life took a step forward so she could notice the "in-between" moments where PTSD wasn't dominating her experiences.

Summary

Paying attention to experiences enables you to reap the rewards of your behavioral activation toward recovery. Practicing mindfulness, a nonjudgmental and present-focused perspective, can deepen your appreciation for the positive experiences in your day and allow you to better coast through the more challenging moments in your day without the need to overcontrol or change difficult emotions. We hope these skills will help you discover that all of your thoughts and emotions are temporary and constantly changing and that if you don't "grab the wheel" or try and swerve away from PTSD symptoms, they will pass more quickly and interrupt your life less frequently.

In the next chapter, we will return to the suggestion to involve others in your behavioral activation toward recovery from PTSD. We dedicate an entire chapter to the idea of involving support people in your recovery because of the potential benefits that we have observed when people reach out to others to help them reach their goals. Remember to use attention to experience skills to observe your mind and all that it tells you when you use your social support network.

CHAPTER 9

Using Social Support to Promote Activation

Human beings are social creatures. Aside from the lone monk or hermit, most of us live in daily relationship with other people and feel that life is more meaningful when we have good relationships. For people with PTSD, relationships can often be complicated and come with potential triggered responses. This can cause people with PTSD to want to withdraw from the world and their relationships. While this is understandable, these patterns undermine social support, which has been found to be the most important predictor of recovery from PTSD (Brewin, Andrews, and Valentine 2000; Ozer et al. 2003).

The term *social support* represents the degree of emotional and practical assistance in your life provided to you by friends and family. Positive and helpful relationships buffer us from stress and help us recover after experiencing traumatic events; this is true across types of trauma exposures, including childhood abuse, military combat, serious accidents, natural disasters, and interpersonal and sexual violence (see Charuvasta and Cloitre 2008). Unfortunately, PTSD has also been shown to erode the quality of social support over time, in part due to PTSD symptoms of irritability and anger, as well as those associated with isolation, avoidance, difficulty trusting others, and emotional numbing (e.g., Benotsch et al. 2000; Ray and Vanstone 2009). For these reasons, we want you to pay attention to the relationships you have in your life and find ways to protect and benefit from your social support networks to promote behavioral activation and recovery from PTSD. If you do not have a strong support network, this can be an important target for your behavioral activation.

Who Are Your Support People?

How would you rate your current level of social support? Is this different from how you would have rated your level of support prior to your trauma? If you feel fairly isolated and cut off from people, you're not alone. Let's first take a look at who is in your life, and then we'll talk about ways to improve your social support.

My Current Social Support Network

Take a moment and make a list of all of the people in your life currently who provide you emotional support or practical help (e.g., helping with chores) or people you *could* count on to help you out of a challenging situation if needed. Start by ranking the people you (could) count on the most often or in the most important ways.

People in my life who (could) provide me support:

1. _____
2. _____
3. _____
4. _____
5. _____
6. _____
7. _____
8. _____
9. _____
10. _____

Now take a moment to think about which of your *top five* social support people can provide you various types of support across situations:

See the examples below.

Person's name and relationship to me: *My best friend Susan*

Provides (or could provide) emotional support? (circle one)   Y   N

If yes, how? If no, why not?

Susan is my "go-to" person when I'm upset. She always has the time to listen to me and gives me encouragement to get through hard times.

Provides (or could provide) practical help in my life?   Y   N

If yes, how? If no, why not?

Susan lives out of state, so it would be hard to ask her for help on small things. But if I needed something "big" she'd be on a plane in a second.

Person's name and relationship to me: *Mike, my brother*

Provides (or could provide) emotional support?   Y   N

If yes, how? If no, why not?

Mike loves me but he's not the first person I'd go to for emotional support. He's more of a "pull yourself up by the bootstraps" kind of guy.

Provides (or could provide) practical help in my life?   Y   N

If yes, how? If no, why not?

Mike helps me all of the time with things like picking up my kids from school if I'm working or helping me stay on top of my car maintenance. If something goes wrong in my house, like a plumbing problem, Mike is always ready to come over and take a look.

Now write about yours.

Person's name and relationship to me: _____

Provides (or could provide) emotional support?   Y   N

If yes, how? If no, why not?

_____

_____

_____

Provides (or could provide) practical help in my life?   Y   N

If yes, how? If no, why not?

_____

_____

_____

Person's name and relationship to me: _____

Provides (or could provide) emotional support?   Y   N

If yes, how? If no, why not?

_____

_____

_____

Provides (or could provide) practical help in my life?   Y   N

If yes, how? If no, why not?

_____

_____

_____

Person's name and relationship to me: _____

Provides (or could provide) emotional support?   Y   N

If yes, how? If no, why not?

_____

_____

_____

Provides (or could provide) practical help in my life?   Y   N

If yes, how? If no, why not?

_____

_____

_____

Person's name and relationship to me: _____

Provides (or could provide) emotional support?   Y   N

If yes, how? If no, why not?

_____

_____

_____

Provides (or could provide) practical help in my life?   Y   N

If yes, how? If no, why not?

_____

_____

_____

Person's name and relationship to me: _____

Provides (or could provide) emotional support?   Y   N

If yes, how? If no, why not?

_____

_____

_____

Provides (or could provide) practical help in my life?   Y   N

If yes, how? If no, why not?

_____

_____

_____

Challenges Asking for Help

We have found that many people (those with and without PTSD) have difficulty asking for help in life. Our individualistic, self-reliant culture tends to champion a "do it yourself" way of being. This may be especially true for many men, military service members, or first responders (e.g., police or firefighters) who, because of masculine or occupational norms, have been taught not to reveal vulnerability or seek help from others for mental health challenges (see Addis and Mahalk 2003; Haguen et al. 2017). Indeed, some of our own research suggests that men who try to adhere to a "tough," go-it-alone mentality generally experience more severe PTSD than those who are more open to asking for help and showing vulnerability (Jakupcak et al. 2014). You may also have difficulty asking for help with PTSD-related difficulties if you feel you "should" be able to do it yourself or "shouldn't" have struggles.

However, people rarely succeed in life without the help and assistance of others, especially when the tasks undertaken are as difficult and complex as recovery from PTSD. And although there may be some "risk" involved in asking others for help, doing so can help the people around you recognize your resilience and the courage you have shown to tackle your PTSD. Read Annie's reflections on her struggles asking for help.

Annie had learned to adjust to being by herself for long periods of time after her first sexual assault trauma in college. She studied alone most of the time and seldom used her professors' office hours for help if she was struggling in a class. Similarly, she mostly worked alone in graduate school and, as she rose through the professional ranks at work, she was more often the person offering help to others than the person seeking out help or support.

Upon reflection, Annie realized her tendencies toward self-reliance were connected with both her PTSD and her family culture. Annie's challenges with trust made it easier for her to figure things out on her own versus ask for help (not trusting that others would be willing to help her without expecting something in return). But Annie also recognized that her parents had instilled a high value placed on independence and stoicism. Her family was of German descent and, combined with their rural farming community values, the cultural stigma associated with being "overly dependent" on others was strongly felt. Annie knew firsthand the downsides to this world view, as she had often felt unsupported emotionally within her family during times of stress. But somehow she had adopted these same views and had come to realize that her fierce independence was a barrier to her recovery from PTSD.

Examining My Challenges Asking for Help

Take a moment to reflect on any difficulties you might have in asking for help and the source of some of these challenges.

Is it difficult for you to ask for help?

_____

_____

_____

Why do you think this is the case?

_____

_____

_____

What are your fears or concerns regarding asking others for help?

_____

_____

_____

_____

Can you imagine some benefits that might come from asking for help?

_____

_____

_____

_____

How Social Support People Can Help

We have laid out some ideas regarding the importance of social support people in your recovery from PTSD and explored challenges you might have seeking support from others. Let's now focus specifically on how you can use social support people to increase the effectiveness of your behavioral activation efforts.

Assistance Refining Your Behavioral Activation Goals

First, as we discussed in chapter 3, we encourage you to talk with social support people in your life about developing your behavioral activation goals. It's important to involve your social support people not just in the beginning of behavioral activation but throughout your recovery, including having discussions with them about what matters most to you (values) and how you are working toward goals and activities that reflect those values. Below are some examples of language and questions you might use to involve them in your goal setting.

- *I have talked to you about having PTSD. I realize it has impacted my relationships with my family. What do you think would be a good first step I could take to reconnect with them?*

- *I realize that some of the stressful events in my life have made it harder for me to stay motivated to exercise regularly. What do you do to motivate yourself to stay healthy?*

- *I'm trying to set some goals for myself to improve my diet. If you were me, where would you start?*

You are likely to use different levels of self-disclosure when you solicit help from your social support people; you might feel comfortable talking with a close friend about your PTSD while feeling disinclined to share your PTSD history with the physical trainer at your gym. That's okay. Not everyone in your life needs to know (or may be able to understand) the impact of PTSD. The important thing is that by inviting others into your goal-setting process, you are enhancing your social support and increasing the likelihood of success in reaching your goals.

Support in Following Through with Your Behavioral Activation Goals

Social support is helpful in choosing and taking initial steps toward your behavioral activation goals. However, involving other people in making sustained progress is even more important. In particular, the people who are part of your day-to-day life are well positioned to provide you support along the way. Take a moment to read about Annie's efforts to involve her social support people in her behavioral activation goal setting.

Annie knew she had difficulty letting other people "in" to her life. Although she loved her daughters very much, she didn't want to share too many details about her PTSD with them, at least not until they were old enough to understand and manage the information she might share. She felt close to her sister but hadn't shared specifics about her traumatic events—she knew she had a sexual trauma history but Annie hadn't volunteered, and her sister hadn't asked more about, what had happened to her. However, Annie recognized that her PTSD symptoms would cause her to isolate (even from her kids) and didn't want to "give in" to the pull away from people. So she decided to talk with her daughters about some of the changes she was making in her life.

Annie shared that she had experienced a lot of "stressful things" in her life that made it hard for her to balance out work and fun. She told her daughters she was determined to take more breaks from chores and to have fun when they were around, and asked if they would join her on her breaks. She designated them as her "fun coaches" and told them she would be open to their suggestions about things she might do to bring more joy into her daily routines. Her daughters loved this assignment. They made suggestions to go bowling, go to movies, and take walks in the nearby park. This helped Annie prioritize fun on weekends. She allowed each of her daughters to suggest one "fun" activity each weekend day. Although they didn't fully appreciative what a positive impact their suggestions had on Annie's life, she felt great satisfaction that her daughters were a central part of her recovery from PTSD.

Can you think of ways that people in your life can help you engage in meaningful and pleasant activities? Complete the exercise below to help you involve your social support people in your weekly activation efforts.

Involving My Support People in My Behavioral Activation Goals

(available at http://www.newharbinger.com/43072)

Fill in the two lists below and answer the question that follows.

This week's behavioral activation target(s):

1. _____

2. _____

3. _____

People who might be able to help me accomplish these tasks:

1. _____

2. _____

3. _____

How could they be helpful? (emotional support, practical support, both?)

_____

_____

_____

Feedback and Positive Reinforcement

Another important way that your social support people can help you make progress with your behavioral activation goals is by offering feedback, both to help you make adjustments if needed and to offer you encouragement (positive reinforcement) for your efforts. You may not always appreciate the results of the changes you are making in in your life, and those people closest to you have the opportunity to reflect back to you the impact of your behavioral activation. It may seem obvious, but having someone give us positive feedback is incredibly helpful in maintaining our motivation for making changes in life.

It would be wonderful if the people in our lives just automatically recognized our efforts and gave us encouragement regularly along the way. However, it is likely that they aren't tracking your efforts as closely as you are and might need some help from you to provide the feedback you are seeking. See below for some example language and questions you might use to solicit feedback.

- *I have been making an effort to reach out to you and other friends more to try and stay better connected with people I care about. From your perspective, has it helped our relationship? Is there anything else I could be doing to bring us closer together?*

- *Remember how I told you I was going to pursue my education goals by signing up for online college classes? It's been going well but it takes a lot of work. I would really appreciate you checking in with me and giving me encouragement along the way until I finish this term.*

- *I really appreciate you going for regular walks with me during the week. Have you noticed any changes in my energy or mood since I began exercising regularly?*

Self-Disclosure

Asking for help sometimes puts you in a place where you need to share details of your struggles with others. This might involve many different levels of self-disclosure. Self-disclosure refers to sharing information about oneself (facts, thoughts, feelings, experiences) and typically leads to greater intimacy. In your recovery from PTSD, you may consider disclosing information about your PTSD symptoms and possibly about your traumatic experience(s), specifically with those to whom you feel closest.

Many of our clients have shared their concerns regarding others' perceptions of them and the "risks" of disclosing their PTSD symptoms. They anticipate that telling others about their

PTSD will cause people to think of them differently, perhaps seeing them as "weak" or becoming afraid or uneasy to spend time with them. Certainly there are stereotypes associated with PTSD. Some people equate having a diagnosis of any psychiatric problem as "being crazy," so it is understandable that one would want to avoid such a label. But it is not accurate. Other people think that people with PTSD are dangerous—that they may hurt others in the middle of a flashback or rage. Such stereotypes do not describe the vast majority of people who have experienced trauma. Furthermore, we have also found that most of the time, our clients' fears about disclosing PTSD to close friends and family aren't predictive of how others will typically react. The stereotypes exist, but many of the people who know and care about you will not characterize your experiences with stereotypes.

We encourage you to share what you are learning about your PTSD with *some* of the closest people in your social support network. You don't necessarily have to go into details about your traumatic events, but letting those around you know (if they don't already) that you are working to overcome PTSD and that PTSD symptoms include irritability, anger, emotional detachment, and tendencies to isolate can help others understand you better (and not take your PTSD symptoms personally), hopefully helping them know you better and be patient with you as you strive to get your life back on track.

There will be people in your social network to whom you might *not* want to disclose your PTSD; that is okay too. But we encourage you to avoid an "all or nothing" rule with regard to sharing your symptoms with people who are important to you. There may be people in your life with whom you spend time who don't need to know anything about your mental health. Some people might only need or want to know that you deal with a lot of "stress." Others might be well positioned to understand the impact of trauma and support you in your recovery from PTSD. Below we talk specifically about trust and PTSD. Consider entrusting others with information about your PTSD as a move away from the isolating downward spiral of PTSD. First, here is an exercise to help you consider self-disclosure in various relationships within your social support network.

Self-Disclosing to People in My Life

Complete the following lists to help you identify who you can self-disclose to at various degrees.

People who would "get it"—These are people I have shared, or could share, select details about my traumatic event(s) with:

1. _____

2. _____

3. _____

People who I would tell I have PTSD—These are people who, although I wouldn't talk about my trauma(s), could understand and support me if I shared I had PTSD:

1. _____

2. _____

3. _____

People who I wouldn't tell I have PTSD but who could support me during times of stress:

1. _____

2. _____

3. _____

People who I wouldn't share my emotions with but who could help distract me or provide practical help in life:

1. _____

2. _____

3. _____

Expanding Your Social Support Network

You might benefit from *expanding* your social support network by seeking out new relationships with people who might be able to support you in your recovery. However, we acknowledge that, for many people with PTSD, this is easier said than done. If this is true for you, consider applying the attention-to-experience and mindfulness skills we discussed in chapter 8 to enhance your engagement in the experience of being with others.

For many people with PTSD, especially those whose traumas are interpersonal in nature (i.e., someone tried to or did cause you harm), developing *trust* and openness with new people is extremely challenging. Past experiences of betrayal and hurt might lead you to conclude, *I'm not going to let people get close enough to me to hurt me again*. Although this is completely understandable, it is one of the core features of PTSD that keep people stuck, isolated, and unable to move ahead with life goals. Here are some points to consider regarding trusting new people to enter into your life.

- Although you may have been hurt by people in your life, not all people in your life want to hurt you.

- You can decide how much and how fast you want to let people get to know you. Developing trust is a process, not a single decision.

- If you *wait* to feel trust toward others before you let them into your life, your PTSD symptoms might keep you waiting for a long time. Like other features of behavioral activation, consider approaching trust from an outside-in perspective…extend trust (in small ways at first) to see how it feels.

- Not all relationships in your life need to be "deep." It's okay to have some people you know casually but with whom you still enjoy doing things.

- When you extend trust to others and let them into your life, you are moving away from the downward spiral of PTSD.

If you were to begin to try and expand your social network, where would you start? Are there specific activities in your community that you might enjoy where you could also potentially meet new people? Do you have existing friendships that would allow you to meet new people (i.e., meeting friends of friends)?

How Can I Expand My Social Network?

(available at http://www.newharbinger.com/43072)

Take a moment to brainstorm ways you might become introduced to new people who might share some of your same interests and values.

Places I could go where I might meet people with whom I could connect:

1. _____
2. _____
3. _____
4. _____
5. _____

Activities I enjoy that might allow me to meet new people:

1. _____
2. _____
3. _____
4. _____
5. _____

Current relationships I have that might introduce me to a wider circle of people:

1. _____
2. _____
3. _____
4. _____
5. _____

Protecting and Enhancing Your Current Social Support Network

As we noted above, research suggests that PTSD symptoms interfere with relationships and erode social support over time (Benotsch et al. 2000; Ray and Vanstone 2009). PTSD symptoms can represent a threat to your social support network by creating tension (e.g., through irritability) or distance (e.g., through mistrust, isolation, or withdrawal) in relationships. One of the most insidious aspects of PTSD is that it tells you to move away from close relationships (or causes others to move away from you), taking away some of your best resources for recovery from PTSD.

Trying to recover from PTSD without social support is like trying to take a road trip across country without using GPS, looking at a map, or stopping to ask for directions; you might still make it but you run the risk of getting very lost along the way. So, how might you strengthen your social support networks and protect relationships so that they aren't negatively impacted from the symptoms of PTSD? First, we encourage you to identify moments where your PTSD symptoms might cause friction with or distance from others. Chances are, you'll find some TRAPs contained in these moments. After all, it is not surprising that one would want to avoid friction. Unfortunately, dealing with interpersonal friction or conflict by avoidance can become a relationship-damaging habit. See if you can find alternative ways of coping with some of your PTSD triggered responses that can help deepen or strengthen your current relationships. In our experience, many people's behavioral activation goals reflect the value and importance of close relationships, so you may have already found yourself applying TRAP/TRAC strategies.

Second, you may need to reach out to develop some additional resources to help you with your relationship skills, like reading or taking classes about effective assertive communication or anger management techniques. It might also mean seeking professional help to address relationship issues. In any case, remember that an investment in your social support network is one of the best things you can do to support your recovery from PTSD.

Read Karl's experience applying TRAP/TRAC strategies to protect and improve some of his closest relationships.

Karl was working hard to improve his relationships, one of his core values and an area in his life he recognized had been significantly changed by his PTSD. Karl noticed that his irritability had a way of "shutting down" his connection with his fiancée. He began to track this pattern and let his fiancée know that he was aware of it. She appreciated that he was taking some initiative to address the pattern, and together they made efforts to observe the irritability and when and why it might arise. After several weeks, they noticed that Karl tended to get irritable on the eve of social events.

Using the TRAP worksheets (see chapter 4), Karl was able to identify that being in social situations tended to trigger some specific war memories of his unit coming under attack in a crowded marketplace square. Karl came to understand that his irritability served as a mask (avoidance) for his trauma-related feelings of worry and anxiety about safety in crowded social situations; when Karl became irritable, it reduced his feelings of vulnerability and made him feel better prepared to respond to any potential threat that might arise.

Karl realized that this pattern wasn't based on a realistic likelihood (he was sure he wouldn't get ambushed at a housewarming party), but the triggered response occurred and he needed to find an alternative way of coping with it. After learning that this triggered response was connected to Karl's irritability, he and his fiancée came up with some strategies to help Karl feel safer in social situations.

They developed a "code word" so Karl could let her know if he was feeling triggered. They talked about who would be at specific gatherings (Karl found this helped reduce his safety concerns). And Karl found that if he worked out an hour or so before a social gathering, he was less likely to get keyed up. The shift from focusing on Karl's irritability to shared problem solving and supportive coping changed the way Karl and his fiancée approached social events and made them feel more like a team.

Summary

The value of social support to your behavioral activation and recovery from PTSD cannot be understated. The single best predictor of recovery from trauma is the presence of positive relationships in your life with people who can offer you emotional support, practical help, or both. The symptoms of PTSD can sometimes erode social support, so we encourage you to proactively take steps to repair, improve, and expand your social networks so that the people who are most important to you can be part of your recovery. Involve others early on in your behavioral activation goal setting and ask for their support throughout the process. Be sure to ask for feedback along the way so your efforts are recognized and reinforced.

In the next chapter we discuss some specific challenges that people with PTSD might encounter using behavioral activation strategies for their recovery. Keep in mind that involving your social support network is a good way to help overcome challenges!

CHAPTER 10

Special Considerations When Using Behavioral Activation for PTSD

We previously discussed how behavioral activation was developed for treating depression and why we thought it would be helpful for people trying to recover their lives after experiencing traumatic events. However, we have noticed through our research and clinical experiences that applying behavioral activation for PTSD may be different from applying it to help overcome depression. In this chapter, we highlight some of our observations and provide suggestions on what to look for and how to adjust your behavioral activation strategies for specific PTSD-related challenges.

Hyperarousal with PTSD

The fifth edition of the *Diagnostic and Statistical Manual of Mental Disorders* (*DSM-5*; APA 2013) classifies PTSD and other trauma-related disorders as distinct from depression and anxiety disorders. However, PTSD was previously classified as an anxiety disorder (APA 2000), in part because the avoidance and hyperarousal symptoms of PTSD shared many of the same features of other anxiety disorders, including fear and avoidance of triggers and elevated appraisal of safety risks. This stands in contrast to depression-related disorders, where low energy and low motivation are often the primary barriers to engagement in life. In other words, depression is like leaving your car parked for weeks at a time because you are low on gas, whereas PTSD is like leaving a car parked because you are afraid you'll crash into something or the engine will explode if you take it out on the open road.

Because of these differences, compared to addressing PTSD, behavioral activation for depression may seem relatively straightforward: start with small activation steps to gather momentum, and seek out pleasure and meaningful experiences to "fill your tank" and give you the encouragement and reinforcement you need to keep driving toward your life goals. Of course, coping with depression is not that easy, and there will be barriers and struggles along the way. Applying behavioral activation for PTSD can be even more complicated due to hyper-arousal (always being on the lookout for threat or danger, even if you aren't aware that you are doing so). It often means you need to anticipate having triggered responses out in the world, learn to cope with these responses, and often develop alternative routes to drive forward toward your life goals.

Furthermore, hyperarousal features of PTSD often include difficulties with anger and aggression as well as impulsive risk-taking behaviors. So in addition to elevated *perceptions* of danger, PTSD symptoms can sometimes actually increase your risk for further exposure to dangerous (and potentially traumatic) events. In fact, we have often noticed that anger, aggression, and risk-taking patterns are actually TRAPs that require both the development of additional coping strategies as well as a solid understanding of what is "driving" these behaviors.

Finally, we have noted that many people with PTSD try and channel their hyperarousal and develop a style that results in "overfunction" in the world; these individuals may adopt what would normally be healthy habits, but take these habits to such extremes that they become problems and barriers to recovery from trauma. Working long hours at a job, exercising at extreme levels, or simply filling your time with chores (e.g., cleaning the house) can cause just as many problems in people's lives as missing work, being inactive, or letting daily tasks build up. These patterns are also often PTSD-related TRAPs that need to be understood and addressed in ways that are different from using behavioral activation for depression.

Both Annie and Karl identified some of the challenges they encountered trying to activate their lives while also dealing with hyperarousal and other PTSD-related symptoms.

Karl: "Sometimes my anger would boil up so quickly and powerfully at work that it would surprise everyone in the room, myself included. It made it more challenging to meet some of my behavioral activation goals related to promotion and leadership because I worried that I might act out and end up losing the respect of my boss."

Annie: "I knew I worked long hours, longer than most of my coworkers, but I didn't really understand what was driving that pattern. However, after several weeks of monitoring my activities and mood, a pattern emerged; I noticed that I tended to work longer hours as a means of avoiding being out in the world, where my PTSD told me I was more likely to be retrauma-tized. It was so exhausting to always be on high alert, so going to work, ironically, became a way to relax."

Identifying the Impact of Hyperarousal

Do you recognize any of these challenges in your life? Do you avoid things because of fear and anxiety (versus simply having low motivation)? Do you tend to engage in conflict (verbal or physical) when out in the world? Have you noticed yourself adopting extreme habits that might seem positive but are done with such excess that they are getting in the way of other important parts of your life? Take a moment and make some notes to help you identify these arousal-related TRAPs.

_____

_____

_____

_____

Do you tend to have fear-related reactions when you are out in the world? What do your fear-related reactions look like to the outside world? How do they feel internally? How do they impact your motivation to accomplish tasks and personal goals?

_____

_____

_____

_____

Do you struggle with irritability, anger, or aggression? Does this ever result in acts of verbal or physical aggression (e.g., yelling, throwing things, getting into physical conflict)? Do you ever use anger to avoid other emotions, such as to mask fear or vulnerability?

_____

_____

_____

_____

Do you sometimes engage in risky behavior (e.g., driving too fast, engaging in unsafe or excessive sexual behavior, using drugs or alcohol to excess)? How does your risk taking impact your motivation to accomplish tasks and personal goals?

_____

_____

_____

_____

Are there behaviors that would normally be healthy or positive but that you take to extreme levels? Have you ever worried that you are acting like a workaholic? Do you tend to fill your time with "busy work" because you have difficulty staying still or to keep painful memories at bay?

_____

_____

_____

_____

Activating "Inwardly" to Navigate Hyperarousal

When we describe behavioral activation to our patients, they tend to assume that we are primarily interested in getting them to go do things in the outside world, such as exercising, socializing, or working toward professional goals. Those certainly are important targets for behavioral activation. However, the challenges we describe above may not be directly helped by doing more. Sometimes, sitting still and paying attention to your internal experiences (thoughts or feelings) is a way of activating more private parts of your life, such as your personal reflections, emotions, or a connection with spirituality or faith.

We have found that helping people with PTSD choose inwardly focused activities helps to balance the pull toward hyperarousal that comes with PTSD. In some ways, activating inwardly allows you to build tolerance for your experiences, as well as practice relaxation and feeling calm so that you can return to those mood states more easily. Here is a partial list of some inwardly focused activation strategies we have found to be useful when helping people recover from PTSD.

Journaling

Sitting quietly in nature

Prayer

Yoga

Hiking

Sitting meditation

Tai chi

Listening to relaxing music

Drawing/painting/adult coloring books

Playing calming music

Here are Karl and Annie's descriptions of using inwardly activating strategies:

Annie: *"I have never been someone who enjoyed running or exercising at a gym. So when I started to focus on my physical health, I went looking for an activity I could do that would promote physical fitness but that would also help me unwind when I wasn't at work. I began taking a noontime yoga class offered at the hospital where I work. It was a little embarrassing at first, because I didn't know what I was doing. But after several months, I noticed that I really looked forward to that noon class. On days when I skipped it, I could tell my stress levels were higher in the afternoon and evening. It also felt good to be moving my body but in a quiet and gentle way, without the overstimulation of the gym and without the anxiety I would have felt if I tried to go running outside."*

Karl: *"Even though my faith is incredibly important to me, I had noticed that my attendance at church fell off after my combat deployment. I'm not sure if it was the crowds at church or if I didn't feel like I had addressed some of the big questions I had about regard to my faith after my traumas. But I found that, if every morning I would read some scripture and pray for ten minutes before I left for the day, the rest of my day tended to go smoother. It has become a way for me to check in with myself and with God before I put myself in the middle of other people and things I need to do."*

My Inward-Acting Behaviors

Take a moment to explore your inward-acting behaviors.

What inward-acting behaviors have you tried?

_____

_____

_____

_____

What inward-acting behaviors are consistent with your values?

_____

_____

_____

_____

What inward-acting behaviors can you commit to trying in the future?

_____

_____

_____

_____

Other Challenging Patterns Common to PTSD

Although these patterns can take many different forms, they often serve the same function: avoidance. We have outlined some of the specific forms of avoidance, often related to hyperarousal, that we have encountered in our clinical work. We ask you to reflect on the specific behaviors below to help you determine which, if any, might be relevant to your PTSD and represent barriers to recovery.

Fear of Anger

Although a negative stereotype exists that suggests that people with PTSD are aggressive and volatile, in fact most people with PTSD do *not* have a history of aggression or violence. However, many of our clients do describe *fearing* intense experiences of anger and worrying that they will lose control over their thoughts or impulses regarding aggressive behaviors. For many of these people, fear of losing control over their anger can become a major obstacle on their road to recovery, because they tend to isolate or withdraw from social situations for fear of acting on their angry thoughts. For these reasons, it can be helpful to know some basic anger-management techniques as well as ways to use mindfulness and clear communication to practice nonaggression when angry.

Many anger-management techniques are simple and commonly known (but less commonly practiced). These include deep breathing exercises to calm your body when frustrated or angry, taking "time outs" and walking away from heated interactions long enough to allow yourself to gather your thoughts and compose what you want to say, and addressing minor frustrations early before they build up to a heated level. It can also be helpful to write about your experiences with anger and review your thoughts and actions so that you can practice communicating your anger in ways that feel healthy and effective.

Attention to experience, or mindfulness (as discussed in chapter 8), can also be an effective tool to manage anger. Simply paying attention to your emotional and physical state will increase your awareness of your anger (or fear of anger) and its impact on your other moods and behaviors. You can also use mindfulness to practice "watching" your anger-related thoughts without feeling you need to take action or judge yourself (or others) harshly.

We also encourage you to do some research to learn the principles of assertive communication. Assertive communication strategies aim to help you link your emotional reaction to specific behaviors or situations, and state to others the reason why you are upset and your preferences to address these frustrations. By practicing talking about your anger in a composed way, you can develop more comfort expressing your irritation or anger effectively in real time, without allowing resentment to build by trying to ignore your anger and without allowing your anger to peak to the point of feeling aggressive or out of control.

Anger-management skills are not formally part of behavioral activation, and you may want or need to find additional resources (books, workshops, or therapy) to help develop these skills. If you do feel that you are at risk of harming yourself or others because of your anger difficulties, you must promptly seek out professional help to keep yourself and your loved ones safe while you work to recover from PTSD.

My Fear of Anger

Take a moment to assess your own fear of anger.

Do you worry about losing control over your anger? Do you go to extreme lengths to avoid feeling angry? Write a little about the fears you have of losing control, what you fear might happen if you do, and what you do to avoid losing control.

_____

_____

_____

Does the fear of losing control over your anger cause you to restrict your life in important ways (e.g., avoiding social situations)? How so?

_____

_____

_____

Firearms and Preparations for Disaster

Safety concerns are common for people with PTSD, many of whom take active steps to improve and ensure their safety and the safety of their loved ones. Sometimes that includes possession of firearms or prepared plans for what to do in case of a natural disaster or other life-threatening event. Although we support your taking basic steps to promote the safety of yourself and your family, we have also noticed than many of the people with PTSD with whom we work can become excessively focused on safety concerns, such that their preparations for disaster begin to eclipse the other valued parts of their life. Often, these extreme safety behaviors are serving as avoidance (e.g., avoiding the experience of vulnerability or fear). It can be useful to understand what is driving these patterns in your life.

When recording your daily activities and mood ratings, notice how often you engage in safety-related thoughts or behaviors, as well as the impact that these behaviors have on your overall mood and well-being. If you can establish basic plans and preparations and turn your attention to other parts of your life, safety concerns may not be a problem. However, if you notice that your preparations become more and more elaborate over time, negatively impact your mood or relationships, or become obstacles to engaging in valued activities, you may want to apply the TRAP/TRAC skills to explore possible alternative ways of coping with triggered responses (e.g., feeling exposed or vulnerable).

My Safety-Related Behaviors

Take a moment to reflect on your safety-related behaviors.

Do you often check your home or environment in repeated patterns (e.g., locking and rechecking locks multiple times)? Describe these patterns.

_____

_____

_____

Do you keep firearms in your house? If so, are they properly stored? Do you carry firearms or other weapons away from your home in order to feel safe? How does your ownership of firearms or weapons create conflict or challenges in your life?

_____

_____

_____

Do you tend to excessively focus on possible disasters, either by continuous preparation or by spending extreme amounts of time researching possible disasters? If so, describe this pattern.

_____

_____

_____

Gambling and Excessive Spending

Many people enjoy gambling as recreation, thrilled by the chance of "winning big." However, there is some research to suggest an association between problematic gambling and

PTSD symptoms (e.g., Green et al. 2017), and we have noticed that some people with PTSD tend to gamble in order to seek out the "adrenaline rush" of winning. We have also noticed that people with PTSD who gamble tend to do so because it allows them to be out in public but minimize social interactions (e.g., playing slot machines). If you gamble, be mindful of what might be driving these behaviors and keep track of any negative consequences (e.g., feeling guilty or angry after losing big sums of money, financial difficulties, relationship problems) that might arise because of your gambling.

My Gambling Behaviors

If you gamble, are you comfortable with the amount of time and money you spend on gambling? Are you chasing the adrenaline high of winning? Has gambling created any difficulties in your relationships or outside life?

_____

_____

_____

Also, we have all been guilty of occasionally but impulsively spending money, often with the hope that whatever we purchase will make us feel happy. Yet we have found that many people with PTSD struggle to keep a balanced budget and often use spending as a means to avoid unpleasant feelings. Does this sound familiar to you?

My Spending Behaviors

What is your relationship with spending money on purchases? Do you ever spend money because of the "rush" of buying something new? Do you feel that you spend more than you can afford? Is there any relationship between your spending and your PTSD symptoms?

_____

_____

_____

Video Games and Social Media

In the past two decades, the popularity of electronic video games and social media platforms has exploded. Many people in our society are expressing concerns about their (or others') excessive use of these forms of entertainment and social communication. Without wading into discussions of the current culture or societal norms, we do want to highlight the risk that people with PTSD may overuse these mediums. Many people with PTSD may be particularly drawn toward these ways of interacting to channel restlessness and because they do not require leaving the home or interacting with unknown people in unfamiliar situations.

If you frequently play video games or spend a significant portion of your leisure time on social media, we encourage you to explore possible TRAPs that might be informing your habits. Do you tend to reach for these outlets when you are feeling anxious or restless? When you complete your activity and mood monitoring worksheets, notice the emotional "costs" that might be involved during extended periods of time online or plugged in.

My Video Game and Social Media Use

How often do you use video games or social media? How does your use of electronic leisure activities cause you problems in relationships or at work?

_____

_____

_____

Pornography and Sex "Addiction"

The *DSM-5* (APA 2013) does not recognize pornography or sex "addiction" as formal disorders. However, people with PTSD may be at elevated risk of compulsively using pornography or seeking out sex. This draw may be related to the patterns of risk-taking or adrenaline-seeking behaviors associated with PTSD. Compulsively engaging in pornography viewing or sexual behaviors may also represent TRAPs, as many people with whom we have worked have described compulsive sex-related behavior as a strategy to "numb" out other emotions.

You likely know best whether your sexual behaviors are a healthy expression of your sexuality or represent a challenge to your recovery from PTSD, but be on alert for negative consequences of pornography or sexual behaviors regarding your mood (e.g., feelings of guilt or shame), relationships, or physical health. If you are struggling with these compulsive patterns, you may benefit from seeking out specific books or support groups to help you find a healthy balance and ensure that PTSD is not driving these patterns.

My Sex-Related Behaviors

Do you worry about the frequency or amount of time you spend looking at pornography or seeking out sex? What PTSD-related TRAPs might be connected with these behaviors?

_____

_____

_____

Obsessive-Compulsive Thoughts and Behaviors

We mentioned above that many behaviors that seem positive can, when done as a means of PTSD avoidance, create problems in life; we have noticed that several of our clients develop patterns of excessive cleaning or a rigid commitment to organization and order. At first pass, this seems like a good thing, but the lives of the people we have worked with became difficult because they focused so much on maintaining a clean and organized environment that other parts of their lives (and the lives of their family and friends) were negatively impacted.

In the same way we encourage you to keep track of your behavioral patterns and moods, we suggest that you observe how and when you engage in cleaning or organizing. Does it often relate to your feeling anxious or upset? Are relationships or other activities negatively impacted? Are you using cleaning as an avoidance strategy to keep memories or other uncomfortable feelings in check? If so, you might need to develop some alternative coping strategies to manage these triggered responses. If you feel unable to change or alter your cleaning behaviors, you may benefit from seeking out cognitive behavioral therapy (CBT) from an experienced mental health professional who specializes in obsessive-compulsive disorder.

My Cleaning and Organizational Behaviors

Have you worried about being compulsive in your habits? How might your cleaning or expectation for organization have caused tension in your relationships or at work?

_____

_____

_____

Excessive Exercise

In our research studies and clinical work, we have found that many individuals who are applying behavioral activation to help recover from PTSD and depression focus on improving their health through regular exercise. In fact, there is some evidence that regular physical exercise can help reduce PTSD symptoms (Rosenbaum et al. 2015). However, some people we have met described extreme exercise patterns that emerged after their exposure to traumatic events.

One of these individuals described working out for three to four hours per day; he was well aware that he was using exercise as an avoidance pattern to keep thoughts of his combat service in check. As a result of his extreme exercise routines, he was regularly injured, which would interfere with his fitness-related goals. For example, despite his desire to compete, he was frequently unable to participate in strength or fitness competitions because of injuries. Another individual we met began competing in ultramarathons (as long as 50 and 100 miles) after her traumatic events; she too recognized that running had come to serve as an avoidance strategy, used to help her isolate socially and suppress memories of her sexual trauma.

Given the general health benefits of regular exercise as well as the evidence that exercise helps reduce PTSD symptoms, we strongly encourage you to consider making health- and wellness-related goals part of your behavioral activation plan. However, be aware of these extreme patterns of exercise. Extreme exercise alone, or exercise paired with unhealthy dieting or food restriction, can develop into an eating disorder and may require specialized treatment.

My Exercise Patterns

If you regularly exercise, do you feel that you are out of control regarding the frequency or duration of your workouts? How can you tell the difference between exercising to feel healthy and exercising to "escape" difficult thoughts and feelings?

_____

_____

_____

Drugs and Alcohol

There is strong and consistent evidence to suggest that people with PTSD are at elevated risk for developing addiction to substances such as nicotine, marijuana, alcohol, or opiates (McCauley et al. 2012). People with PTSD may start out using drugs or alcohol to "self-medicate" their symptoms, such as drinking heavily at night to suppress nightmares and fall asleep. Others may find that they come to rely on drugs or alcohol to be in public or social situations, trying to dampen down feelings of hyperarousal. Others still may find that they struggle to feel positive emotions such as love or happiness without using substances. Unfortunately, these self-medication patterns can quickly evolve into full-blown addiction.

My Patterns of Substance Use

If you drink alcohol, we encourage you to be very mindful of what might be driving your consumption. Do you use alcohol to "calm down" if you are feeling anxious? When you drink socially, are you enhancing a positive experience or relying on alcohol in order to participate? Do you feel in control over your drinking?

_____

_____

_____

If you are using illegal substances, what is the relationship between your PTSD and drug use? For example, are you self-medicating your PTSD with these substances?

_____

_____

_____

Summary

There are many other behaviors that may function as avoidance with PTSD, impede your recovery from PTSD, and cause additional problems in your life, including over- or undereating, sleeping too much or keeping yourself up at night, or frequent moving ("geographical relocations"). We encourage you to reflect on your own behavior and consider whether there may be any additional TRAPs for you to address.

In behavioral activation we typically focus on behaviors you would like to *increase*, to reduce avoidance and improve your quality of life. However, it is also the case that many people with PTSD engage in behaviors in order to cope with or reduce (that is, avoid) PTSD symptoms; therefore, targets of behavioral activation for PTSD may also be behaviors to *decrease*. In this chapter we overviewed many common problems that people with PTSD manifest as they try to cope with their arousal and other trauma-related symptoms. While the form of avoidance may change from person to person, the underlying function is often the same—an attempt to avoid the negative memories, feelings, and experiences that they associate with their traumatic events.

A behavioral activation approach to treating PTSD starts with understanding what drives the behaviors and focuses on promoting positive alternatives to these less adaptive patterns. If you aren't able to use the TRAP/TRAC method to successfully change any of the behaviors discussed above (or patterns not listed but known to you), we encourage you to seek out additional resources, including books, workshops, and direct care from a qualified mental health professional.

CHAPTER 11

Summary and Relapse Prevention

Congratulations on working your way through *The PTSD Behavioral Activation Workbook*! We hope you have seen that you can break out of the downward spiral of your PTSD and instead focus on rebuilding a life of value and meaning. However, we do not expect that your life is exactly what you want it to be or that you have completely resolved your PTSD by now. We *do* hope that you have been able to jump-start your recovery from PTSD and put your life back on the road toward achieving your personal goals.

In fact, a central assumption of behavioral activation for PTSD is that you will continue to develop and hone the skills you have learned so far, putting them to use as you advance toward your current goals and set new goals for your future. Consider this workbook to be an initial set of directions toward your recovery from PTSD but not the complete road map for the entirety of your life. Indeed, we hope that you practice the core skills of behavioral activation for the rest of your life, constantly orienting toward new goals and improved quality of life. To review, the core skills of behavioral activation for PTSD are:

- Identify personal values and set specific goals for the future.

- Break down large goals into smaller subgoals.

- Take steps toward your goals.

- Identify TRAPs (trigger, response, avoidance-patterns) that might divert you from your goals.

- Experiment with TRAC (trigger, response, alternative coping) strategies to make progress toward your goals.

- Use creative problem-solving skills to overcome practical barriers to making progress toward your goals.

- Practice "attention to experience" and mindfulness skills to foster present-moment, nonjudgmental awareness of your experiences as you have them.

- Use your social support network to help you set and make progress toward your goals.

It may be helpful to reread the workbook several times as you learn to apply these core skills. Go back to specific chapters covering topics that you find challenging or that seem to be working especially well in your use of behavioral activation. You might find it particularly helpful to review your responses to the exercises in each chapter and notice any changes in how you would respond in the present moment.

In fact, we'd like you to review the previous chapters now and make a note of one thing that you learned or that stood out for you in each one. Particularly, think about something that was relevant to you and for which the chapter helped you apply an idea, strategy, or practice to your own life. Let's call these your chapter "take-home points."

Take-Home Points

(available at http://www.newharbinger.com/43072)

List one take-home point for each chapter here.

Chapter 1. _____

_____

_____

Chapter 2. _____

_____

_____

Chapter 3. _____

_____

_____

Chapter 4. _____

_____

_____

Chapter 5. _____

_____

_____

Chapter 6. _____

_____

_____

Chapter 7. _____

_____

_____

Chapter 8. _____

_____

_____

Chapter 9. _____

_____

_____

Chapter 10. _____

_____

_____

We also want to encourage you to practice these behavioral activation skills every day. Make note of when you use specific skills and in what situations. Tracking both your use of behavioral activation skills and the impact on your life helps you get better and better at using behavioral activation to recover from PTSD.

Take ACTION Every Day

The more you use behavioral activation, the more it will become second nature. We have proposed that you use the acronyms TRAP and TRAC to help monitor your avoidance patterns and develop alternative ways of coping. We have one more acronym that may prove useful to you as you establish new habits of activation and reengagement in life: ACTION (Jacobson et al. 2001). It stands for a series of steps you can use every day to evaluate the benefits (and potential challenges) you face in your use of behavioral activation for PTSD. The steps are as follows:

A: Assess. Take a moment to assess a specific situation. Notice any PTSD symptoms present and any pull toward avoidance that may take you off course from your recovery goals.

C: Choose. Consider how you might respond to a specific situation. This might involve employing multiple alternative coping strategies or it might involve choosing avoidance. Just make sure you pay attention to your choice (that is, don't do it automatically—instead register that you are choosing a particular response).

T: Try. Try out your response. See if it helps your mood or worsens it. Notice how it feels to be using a particular response. Watch to see what short-term outcomes might be associated with your choice. If you feel stress (which can happen with behavioral activation for PTSD), also notice if it got you closer to your long-term goals.

I: Integrate. If you feel positive about a particular response to a situation, make it part of your routine. By doing so, you will have a chance to practice this response in many different situations and over time.

O: Observe. Now that you have tried out a specific response to a situation over time, take a step back and look at the broader impact of this type of response. Are you happy with the outcomes? If you imagine this response being a regular part of your routine, do you feel positive about the long-term outcomes that it might bring?

N: Never give up. If you have observed positive outcomes from your chosen response, continue to practice it. If you aren't satisfied with your response and what it yields, go back to the assessment phase, choose a different response, try it out, integrate it into your routine, and observe the consequences of this second choice.

Applying the ACTION processes to your daily life can help you take behavioral activation skills beyond a single moment in time and extend your efforts in order to create a habit of behavioral activation.

Take Regular "Big Picture" Self-Assessments

To support a lifelong application of behavioral activation, we also encourage you to adopt a habit of regularly stepping back from your life and immediate experience of PTSD symptoms to more *globally* assess your personal progress toward your behavioral activation goals.

Some of our clients have adopted a monthly practice of reviewing their symptoms, their values, their progress toward specific goals, and their use of problem-solving strategies to help them advance toward the next level in their recovery from PTSD.

Below is an example of a monthly review exercise you might employ to help make behavioral activation a lifelong habit.

Monthly Behavioral Activation for PTSD Self-Assessment

(available at http://www.newharbinger.com/43072)

PTSD Symptom Review

This past month, I noticed the following changes in the frequency and/or intensity of my PTSD symptoms in comparison to when I started behavioral activation. (Circle the best answer.)

Nightmares

Increase   Decrease   No Change

Intrusive thoughts

Increase   Decrease   No Change

Emotional reactivity to triggers

Increase   Decrease   No Change

Physiological (body) reactivity to triggers

Increase   Decrease   No Change

Flashbacks

Increase   Decrease   No Change

Avoidance of trauma-related thoughts, memories, or feelings

Increase   Decrease   No Change

Avoidance of external reminders (triggers) of my trauma

Increase   Decrease   No Change

Inability to remember important aspects of the traumatic event

Increase   Decrease   No Change

Negative views of myself or the world

Increase   Decrease   No Change

Unrealistic blame of myself or others related to my trauma

Increase   Decrease   No Change

Persistent negative emotions (e.g., shame, guilt, anger, fear)

Increase   Decrease   No Change

Low levels of interest in or enjoyment of activities

Increase   Decrease   No Change

Social Isolation and emotional detachment from others

Increase   Decrease   No Change

Difficulties feeling positive emotions (e.g., love, joy)

Increase   Decrease   No Change

Irritability or aggression

Increase   Decrease   No Change

Self-destructive or risky behaviors

Increase   Decrease   No Change

Hypervigilance related to safety

Increase   Decrease   No Change

Startle (jumpy) reactions

Increase   Decrease   No Change

Problems with concentration

Increase   Decrease   No Change

Problems falling or staying asleep

Increase   Decrease   No Change

Notes related to changes in PTSD symptoms:

_____

_____

_____

_____

Review of TRAPs

This month, I identified the following TRAPs in my daily routines.

1. _____

2. _____

3. _____

Notes related to my identified TRAPs:

_____

_____

_____

_____

This month, I tried to use the following TRAC strategies.

1. _____

2. _____

3. _____

Notes related to my identified TRAC strategies:

_____

_____

_____

_____

Review of Values and Goals

In the past month, my personal goals were related to the following personal values.

1. _____

2. _____

3. _____

My specific goals included the following:

1. _____

2. _____

3. _____

Satisfaction with Progress

My satisfaction with my progress for Goal 1 was

Very satisfied   Satisfied   Neutral   Dissatisfied   Very Dissatisfied

Notes on satisfaction with progress for Goal 1:

_____

_____

_____

My satisfaction with my progress for Goal 2 was

Very satisfied   Satisfied   Neutral   Dissatisfied   Very Dissatisfied

Notes on satisfaction with progress for Goal 2:

_____

_____

_____

My satisfaction with my progress for Goal 3 was

Very satisfied   Satisfied   Neutral   Dissatisfied   Very Dissatisfied

Notes on satisfaction with progress for Goal 3:

_____

_____

_____

Review of Challenges and Barriers

I experienced the following challenges making progress for Goal 1.

_____

_____

_____

I experienced the following challenges making progress for Goal 2.

_____

_____

_____

I experienced the following challenges making progress for Goal 3.

_____

_____

_____

Review of Problem-Solving Strategies

This month, I tried the following problem-solving strategies to overcome practical barriers to my goals.

1. _____

2. _____

3. _____

Next month, my top three goals are the following (you can choose to either continue to work on a prior goal and or set a new goal).

Goal 1: _____

Goal 2: _____

Goal 3: _____

We recognize that we've just provided you with a number of things to review and write. Always keep in mind the strategy to break things down into doable steps or tasks. You can spend time with just one of these "big picture" activities before moving on to the next if the whole feels overwhelming. There is no rush. We have used metaphors of cars and traveling throughout, and in keeping with that metaphor, you can use this workbook like you would use the owner's manual to your car (although we hope it won't just sit in a glovebox under a pile of service receipts!). Nobody reads and memorizes the owner's manual for a car, but they do familiarize themselves with the various sections. Then they return to a section when necessary to troubleshoot a problem that occurs or to learn how to do something with the car that doesn't routinely occur, like how to locate the window washer fluid when it is time to refill. Hang onto this workbook as you put behavioral activation into action, and return to it when you need reminders.

Expect and Respond to Stalls and Setbacks

Although we want to help you maintain and advance your progress, we also want to prepare you for what may likely be a zigzag path toward recovery from PTSD. There may be several times when you feel stalled in your progress. This may look like a period of low motivation, or it might involve several start-and-stop efforts where you feel as though you aren't making the headway you had hoped. Please keep in mind that these are normal parts of the change process. Indeed, we fully expect that you may make several attempts toward behavioral activation in one or more areas of your life before you gain enough momentum to experience consistent progress.

Furthermore, you may find that you make great progress in one or more areas, but for one reason or another, you gravitate back to TRAPs. Often, outside stressful events (e.g., work, finances, health issues, or relationship problems) can disrupt new routines and point you back toward the downward spiral of PTSD. Rather than seeing this as a failure, we encourage you to expect this as a natural part of change. For most of us, it takes several attempts to change our behavior before we establish new, more positive habits and routines.

Occasionally, an effort toward behavioral activation can lead to a negative outcome—like having a severe panic attack or an angry outburst that leads to an altercation. While this is rare, when it occurs it is easy to fall back into TRAPs. However, it is important to approach yourself with compassion and see this as useful information. That is, rather than signifying a failure or evidence that you can't do a task, this represents the need to step back and assess what happened. Likely the step was too big or there were circumstances you didn't anticipate. Now, with this information, you can plan ahead and problem solve how you might get through a similar situation more effectively in the future. In order to do this successfully, you must first be able to identify these stalls and setbacks, and then prepare to respond. Let's look at these steps more closely.

Identify Stalls and Setbacks

As with the other behavioral activation strategies, we believe that an important part of the change process is developing an *awareness* of when you are feeling stalled out in your progress, or even experiencing some setbacks that leave you feeling as though you are losing ground in your progress toward your goals. However, it is sometimes difficult to know when we have stalled out in our progress or are falling back into older patterns. Here are some questions you can ask yourself regularly to catch times when you have plateaued or lost ground on your behavioral activation road to recovery:

1. Have I taken any new steps toward my goals in the past week? If not, is this because of low motivation or other practical barriers? Has my mood or self-esteem changed as a result of this static pattern?

2. Am I choosing TRAPs more than I am trying out new TRAC strategies? Am I prioritizing the avoidance of stress (or triggered responses) over the advancement of my personal values and goals?

3. Have I felt as though I am on "autopilot" or "checked out" from my daily activities? Is this because I am less interested in or place less value on my current activities?

These are good general questions to help you identify stalls and setbacks, but you probably have some awareness of signs that are specific to you and your PTSD. Read about the signs Annie identified as indications of being stalled out or experiencing setbacks in her progress toward recovery:

- "I know I've hit a wall in my progress when I'm bored."

- "I know I've stalled in my behavioral activation when I stop tracking my activities and their connections to my moods."

- "I can tell I'm spinning my wheels when I haven't set a new goal for myself in more than two weeks."

- "When I get irritable or negative in my thinking, it's often a sign that I've lost focus on my behavioral activation goals."

- "If I haven't been somewhere new or interacted with a person outside of my small circle of family and friends for more than two weeks, it's a good indicator that I've stalled in my recovery."

Annie identified the following signs of setbacks or slips back into old TRAP patterns:

- "When I repeatedly say no to invitations to go out to public places, I know I am starting to isolate."

- "When I start to stay late at work more than one or two nights per week, I know I'm starting to use work as an avoidance strategy."

- "When my fear of anxiety or panic outweighs my values regarding where I will go and what I will do with my day, I know I'm having a setback."

- "When I watch TV more than two hours per day, I'm probably engaging in avoidance patterns."

- "When I start to worry about things in the future for more than a few minutes at a time, I'm likely not using my mindfulness skills to stay present and focused on what is in front of me."

Of course, your signals of being stalled or slipping back into old TRAPs may look very different from Annie's. Complete the following exercise to identify your signs.

My Signs of Stalls or Setbacks

(available at http://www.newharbinger.com/43072)

Take a moment and make a list of signs that you will recognize to help you identify periods of stagnation or retreat from your progress.

Signs I have become stalled in my progress:

1. _____
2. _____
3. _____
4. _____
5. _____

Signs I am falling back into old TRAPs:

1. _____
2. _____
3. _____
4. _____
5. _____

Identifying these patterns of stagnation or retreat from behavioral activation is an important first step. However, it is also important that you develop a plan for how to respond to these stalls and setbacks so that you are ready to respond to them when they arise.

Prepare to Respond to Stalls and Setbacks

Although we expect you to have days, weeks, or even months where you feel like you have hit a plateau or fallen back into old TRAP cycles, with some preparation, you can help ensure that these don't take you fully out of your path toward recovery. The following general strategies have proven to be helpful for many of our clients using behavioral activation for PTSD in order to maintain and or reestablish momentum when they have stalled out or experienced setbacks:

- Maintain regular check-ins with your progress toward your goals (such as the monthly assessment above); this will allow you to identify stalls and setbacks early on and reorient you toward your behavioral activation goals.

- Give yourself permission to try out some of your old TRAPs, but take careful notes on how the avoidance impacts your mood and outlook. Often, using avoidance on purpose can help you better see the "costs" involved and help you restart your path toward recovery.

- When you feel stalled or are falling back into TRAP cycles, talk to one or more of your social support people. Let them know you've lost some forward momentum and ask for their advice or help getting back on TRAC.

- Remember that each challenge to your use of behavioral activation for PTSD is an opportunity for learning and practice. Adopt the "curious mind" of a mechanic and analyze where things got off track for you. When you restart your behavioral activation strategies for a specific goal, pay attention and take notes on what worked last time and what didn't.

- If you have stalled out or had setbacks in one domain of your life and are having trouble restarting your behavioral activation action steps for a specific goal, consider refocusing on another important domain of your life and set some new goals. Keep in mind that you can always return to a behavioral activation goal at a different time.

Annie developed a list of specific strategies she could use to respond to the signs of stalls or setbacks she had listed. Here are some of her strategies:

- "When I feel bored or irritable, I recognize these as signs of being stalled out—I go back and read my lists of personal values. It sometimes helps me get motivated again and I'll try to focus on taking one or more new action steps toward a new goal in the week ahead."

- "When I haven't been somewhere new or interacted with a person outside of my inner circle for a couple of weeks, I force myself to go out in public. I either go somewhere I haven't been before or I go somewhere familiar but force myself to talk to at least two different people. Even if I only say 'hi' to someone working in a store, it helps me stay out of isolation."

- "I have a program on my TV that tracks how many hours I view each day. Whenever it goes above two hours, I tell myself that I need to choose a different activity. Ideally, I choose something related to my behavioral activation goals."

Now take a moment to develop some strategies for your own signs of stalls or setbacks.

My Strategies for Responding to Stalls or Setbacks

(available at http://www.newharbinger.com/43072)

Apply what you've learned about dealing with stalls and setbacks to complete this exercise.

When I notice one or more of the signs of stagnation or setbacks that I listed above, I can try the following strategies to get back on TRAC:

1. _____
2. _____
3. _____
4. _____
5. _____

Think Long Term

We have suggested that you set specific goals (aligned with your personal values) and take a series of action steps toward these goals to gather momentum and advance toward an improved quality of life. Typically, our clients have planned these action steps for the weeks or months ahead with the aim of achieving some personal goal within the next six months to a year. We strongly encourage you to stay focused on these more immediate action steps and goals when you begin to learn and apply behavioral activation for PTSD. However, as you begin to make progress and become familiar with these behavioral activation strategies, you will be well positioned to set your sights on long-term goals. Below are a series of questions designed to help you both assess your more immediate goals and also plan ahead to achieve longer-term success.

My Long-Term Goals

(available at http://www.newharbinger.com/43072)

I have set the following goals within the past month:

1. _____

2. _____

3. _____

In the next six months, I'd like to make significant progress toward these goals:

1. _____

2. _____

3. _____

In the next year, I'd like to make significant progress toward these goals:

1. _____

2. _____

3. _____

In five years from now, I'd like to achieve (or make significant progress toward) these goals:

1. _____

2. _____

3. _____

If you find that it is helpful to make even longer-term goals, continue this exercise (e.g., "In the next ten years…"). However, keep in mind that your values and goals may shift over time. It is perfectly acceptable to revisit these goals and make changes along the way. Also ask yourself if any changes in your goals are related to PTSD avoidance (versus changes reflective of your pursuit of a quality life).

Anticipate and Prepare for Future Stressors

Everyday stressful events, such as car troubles, relationship challenges, or health issues, are likely to exacerbate your PTSD symptoms. So even if you have made excellent progress using behavioral activation for PTSD, it is likely that different life challenges will put you back on your heels and invite stalls or setbacks. It is also possible that you will experience other types of traumatic events. No matter how good we become at taking action to create a meaningful and positive life for ourselves, the possibility of suddenly losing a loved one, experiencing a crisis in our health, or encountering new traumatic experiences exists.

At first pass, this may seem like a pessimistic or discouraging viewpoint. However, we bring it up here because, in our experience, these challenges will find most of us sooner or later. With or without PTSD, situations like these will invite all of us to either retreat into avoidance or learn to overcome adversity and demonstrate resiliency. Obviously, we hope and expect that your knowledge and practice of behavioral activation is excellent preparation for these types of future stressors. Remember that we first applied behavioral activation as a treatment for PTSD because the skills resemble the types of adaptive and healthy coping strategies that allow people to overcome traumatic events.

So consider your behavioral activation skill set to be a resource to overcome past traumas and face (and overcome) future stressors, including future traumatic events. Staying connected with your personal values, oriented toward your future goals, and attentive to your daily activities and how they improve (or don't improve) your mood will put you in a good place to stay on course no matter what comes your way.

Final Thoughts

We have written this workbook in the hopes that you can learn to break free of the downward spiral of PTSD and begin to rebuild a meaningful life, reflective of your personal values and oriented toward recovery from PTSD. We also know how powerful PTSD can be and the substantial "pull" of avoidance that will arise again and again in your life. So we wish that you can undertake this journey with a stance of self-compassion, humor, and patience for yourself as you reclaim your life from the effects of trauma.

We also firmly believe that, although self-guided recovery is possible and a powerful approach to overcoming PTSD, seeking out mental health services can bolster your efforts and provide you important support and guidance along the way. If you are already in therapy or plan on seeking out therapy in the near future, please share these strategies with your therapist and let them know that you would like their help using behavioral activation to address your PTSD. We also encourage you to be open to other psychotherapies and treatment approaches that can be used in conjunction with behavioral activation for PTSD. As we mentioned in the beginning of this workbook, there is very strong evidence to suggest that psychotherapies that help you process your traumatic memories can be extremely helpful and reduce PTSD symptoms significantly. Be sure to find a therapist who has training and experience in evidence-based approaches to treating PTSD so that you can be certain they have the expertise to guide you through the processing of your traumatic experiences. We also encourage you to consider talking with a qualified medical provider about specific medications that might help you improve your sleep and manage some of the more extreme emotions that come with PTSD.

Lastly, we want to share with you our sense of hopefulness with regard to your recovery from PTSD. Our research studies and the work of other researchers suggest that this straightforward approach can have powerful effects in changing your PTSD and improving your quality of life. Indeed, we have worked with individuals who, when we first met them, were homeless and entangled in the legal system; these same people used behavioral activation to start their recovery from PTSD and went on to earn graduate degrees (one became a lawyer, another went to medical school). Some of our clients have used behavioral activation to reclaim their physical health and compete in marathons after losing limbs during combat tours. Others have used behavioral activation strategies to build businesses. Our clients have used behavioral activation to develop healthy and rewarding relationships and become better parents, and several have entered into social service careers to become treatment providers or advocates to help others who have experienced trauma and PTSD.

None of these people accomplished these things in a few months, but all of them began by using the strategies we have outlined in the book to jump-start their recovery from PTSD. We are confident that you can achieve the important goals that you set for yourself by taking action step after action step until you have developed new habits for living and found ways to sidestep the TRAPs of PTSD.

So take ACTION toward your recovery. If (when) you become stalled out or experience setbacks, step back and adopt a curious mind about what is and is not working. Try different approaches to meeting your goals. Remain creative when problem solving around any challenges that arise. Involve others in your recovery. Remain self-compassionate and try to find humor, even in the more challenging moments of your recovery. And finally, don't give up and don't give in to your PTSD. Choose the life you want and pursue it!

Daily Activity and Mood Monitoring Chart

Time	Mon	Tues	Wed	Thurs	Friday	Sat	Sun
6A–8A	Activity Mood	Activity Mood	Activity Mood	Activity Mood	Activity Mood	Activity Mood	Activity Mood
8A–10A	Activity Mood	Activity Mood	Activity Mood	Activity Mood	Activity Mood	Activity Mood	Activity Mood
10A–12P	Activity Mood	Activity Mood	Activity Mood	Activity Mood	Activity Mood	Activity Mood	Activity Mood
12P–2P	Activity Mood	Activity Mood	Activity Mood	Activity Mood	Activity Mood	Activity Mood	Activity Mood
2P–4P	Activity Mood	Activity Mood	Activity Mood	Activity Mood	Activity Mood	Activity Mood	Activity Mood
4P–6P	Activity Mood	Activity Mood	Activity Mood	Activity Mood	Activity Mood	Activity Mood	Activity Mood

6P–8P	Activity Mood	Activity Mood	Activity Mood	Activity Mood	Activity Mood	Activity Mood	Activity Mood
8P–10P	Activity Mood	Activity Mood	Activity Mood	Activity Mood	Activity Mood	Activity Mood	Activity Mood
10P–12A	Activity Mood	Activity Mood	Activity Mood	Activity Mood	Activity Mood	Activity Mood	Activity Mood
12A–2A	Activity Mood	Activity Mood	Activity Mood	Activity Mood	Activity Mood	Activity Mood	Activity Mood
TRAPs during the day	1. 2. 3.	1. 2. 3.	1. 2. 3.	1. 2. 3.	1. 2. 3.	1. 2. 3.	
Costs of Avoidance							

References

Addis, M. E., and J. R. Mahalik. 2003. "Men, Masculinity, and the Context of Help Seeking." *The American Psychologist* 58: 5–14.

American Psychiatric Association. 2000. *Diagnostic and Statistical Manual of Mental Disorders, 4th ed., text rev.* Washington, DC: Author.

American Psychiatric Association. 2013. *Diagnostic and Statistical Manual of Mental Disorders, 5th ed.* Washington, DC: Author.

Asmundson, G. J., M. J. Coons, S. Taylor, and J. Katz. 2002. "PTSD and the Experience of Pain: Research and Clinical Implications of Shared Vulnerability and Mutual Maintenance Models." *Canadian Journal of Psychiatry* 47: 930–937.

Benotsch, E. G., K. Brailey, J. J. Vasterling, M. Uddo, J. I. Constans, and P. B. Sutker. 2000. "War Zone Stress, Personal and Environmental Resources, and PTSD Symptoms in Gulf War Veterans: A Longitudinal Study." *Journal of Abnormal Psychology* 109: 205–213.

Boyd, J. E., R. A. Lanius, and M. C. McKinnon. 2018. "Mindfulness-Based Treatments for Posttraumatic Stress Disorder: A Review of the Treatment Literature and Neurobiological Evidence." *Journal of Psychiatry & Neuroscience 43*: 7–25.

Brewin, C. R., B. Andrews, and J. D. Valentine. 2000. "Meta-analysis of Risk Factors for Posttraumatic Stress Disorder in Trauma-Exposed Adults." *Journal of Consulting and Clinical Psychology* 68: 748–766.

Charuvastra, A., and M. Cloitre. 2008. "Social Bonds and Posttraumatic Stress Disorder." *Annual Review of Psychology, 59*: 301–328.

Craske, M. G. 2012. "Transdiagnostic Treatment for Anxiety and Depression." *Depression and Anxiety* 29: 749–753.

Dimidjian, S., M. Barrera Jr, C. Martell, R. F. Munoz, and P. M. Lewinsohn. 2011. "The Origins and Current Status of Behavioral Activation Treatments for Depression." *Annual Review of Clinical Psychology* 7: 1–38.

Goldberg, S. B., R. P. Tucker, P. A. Greene, R. J. Davidson, B. E. Wampold, D. J. Kearney, and T. L. Simpson. 2018. "Mindfulness-Based Interventions for Psychiatric Disorders: A Systematic Review and Meta-analysis." *Clinical Psychology Review* 59: 52–60.

Green, C. L., R. W. Nahhas, A. A. Scogilio, and I. Elman. 2017. "Post-Traumatic Stress Symptoms in Pathological Gambling: Potential Evidence of Anti-Reward Processes." *Journal of Addictive Behavior* 6: 98–101.

Haguen, P. T., A. M. McGrillis, G. E. Smid, and M. J. Nijdam. 2017. "Mental Health Stigma and Barriers to Mental Health Care for First Responders: A Systematic Review and Meta-analysis." *Journal of Psychiatric Research* 94: 218–229.

Hoge, C. W., and K. M. Chard. 2018. "A Window into the Evolution of Trauma-Focused Psychotherapies for Posttraumatic Stress Disorder." *Journal of the American Medical Association* 319: 343–345.

Iacoviello, B. M., G. Wu, R. Abend, J. W. Murrough, A. Feder, E. Fruchter, Y. Levenstein, et al. 2014. "Attention Bias Variability and Symptoms of Posttraumatic Stress Disorder." *Journal of Traumatic Stress* 27: 232–239.

Imel, Z. E., K. Laska, M. Jakupcak, and T. L. Simpson. 2013. "Meta-analysis of Dropout in Treatments for Posttraumatic Stress Disorder." *Journal of Consulting and Clinical Psychology* 81 (3): 394–404. doi: 10.1037/a0031474

Jacobson, N. S., C. R. Martell, and S. Dimidjian. 2001. "Behavioral Activation Treatment for Depression: Returning to Contextual Roots." *Clinical Psychology: Science and Practice* 8: 255–270.

Jakupcak, M., R. K. Blais, J. Grossbard, H. Garcia, and J. Okiishi. 2014. "'Toughness' in Association with Mental Health Symptoms Among Iraq and Afghanistan War Veterans Seeking Veteran Affairs Health Care." *Psychology of Men and Masculinity* 15: 100–104.

Jakupcak, M., A. Wagner, A. Paulson, A. Varra, and M. McFall. 2010. "Behavioral Activation as a Primary Care-Based Treatment for PTSD and Depression Among Returning Veterans." *Journal of Traumatic Stress* 23: 491–495.

Kabat-Zinn, J. (1994). *Wherever You Go, There You Are: Mindfulness Meditation in Everyday Life.* New York: Hyperion.

McCauley, J. L., T. Killeen, D. F. Gros, K. T. Brady, and S. E. Back. 2012. "Posttraumatic Stress Disorder and Co-occurring Substance Use Disorders: Advances in Assessment and Treatment." *Clinical Psychology* 19.

Ono, M., G. J. Devilly, and D. Shum. 2016. "A Meta-analytic Review of Overgeneral Memory: The Role of Trauma, Mood, and the Presence of Posttraumatic Stress Disorder." *Psychological Trauma Theory Research Practice and Policy* 8: 157–164.

Ozer, E. J., S. R. Best, T. L. Lipsey, and D. S. Weiss. 2003. "Predictors of Posttraumatic Stress Disorder and Symptoms in Adults: A Meta-analysis." *Psychological Bulletin* 129: 52–73.

Ray, S. L., and M. Vanstone. 2009. "The impact of PTSD on Veterans' Family Relationships: An Interpretive Phenomenological Inquiry." *International Journal of Nursing Studies* 46: 838–847.

Rosenbaum, S., D. Vancampfort, Z. Steel, J. Newby, P. B. Ward, and B. Stubbs. 2015. "Physical Activity in the Treatment of Post-Traumatic Stress Disorder: A Systematic Review and Meta-analysis." *Psychiatry Research* 230: 130–136.

Schottenbauer, M. A., C. R. Glass, D. B. Arnkoff, V. Tendick, and S. H. Gray. 2008. "Nonresponse and Dropout Rates in Outcome Studies on PTSD: Review and Methodological Considerations." *Psychiatry* 71 (2): 134–68. doi: 10.1521/psyc.2008.71.2.134

Wagner, A. W., D. F. Zatzick, A. Ghesquiere, and G. J. Jurkovich. 2007. "Behavioral Activation as an Early Intervention for Posttraumatic Stress Disorder and Depression Among Physically Injured Trauma Survivors." *Cognitive and Behavioral Practice* 14: 341–349.

Matthew Jakupcak, PhD, is a clinical psychologist and researcher who has studied and treated psychological trauma, post-traumatic stress disorder (PTSD), and high-risk behaviors in military veterans, first responders (i.e., firefighters, paramedics, police officers), and young adults. Jakupcak is an associate professor at the University of Washington School of Medicine, and has published more than fifty peer-reviewed scientific articles and book chapters, and presented at over sixty national and regional conferences and workshops on the topics of PTSD, depression, suicidal behaviors, interpersonal violence, and behavioral activation treatment interventions in trauma-exposed populations. He lives in Missoula, MT.

Amy Wagner, PhD, is a clinical psychologist with the PTSD Clinical Team at the VA Portland Health Care System, and associate professor at Oregon Health and Science University. She specializes in cognitive-behavioral treatments for PTSD, and dialectical behavior therapy (DBT); and holds a part-time practice with a focus on the treatment of PTSD and related disorders. She has published numerous articles on PTSD, and, with Matthew Jakupcak, completed the first randomized clinical trial of behavioral activation for the treatment of PTSD.

Christopher R. Martell, PhD, ABPP, is a licensed psychologist, and is board certified in clinical, behavioral, and cognitive psychology through the American Board of Professional Psychology. He is clinic director of the Psychological Services Center, and lecturer at the University of Massachusetts Amherst. Martell has coauthored eight books, and has authored or coauthored numerous articles and chapters on behavioral activation.

Foreword writer **Matthew T. Tull, PhD**, is professor in the department of psychology at the University of Toledo. Tull's research is focused on the role of emotion regulation difficulties in the development and maintenance of PTSD, as well as maladaptive behaviors (e.g., substance use) that often occur in the context of PTSD.

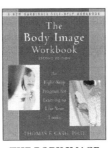

Register your **new harbinger** titles for additional benefits!

When you register your **new harbinger** title—purchased in any format, from any source—you get access to benefits like the following:

- Downloadable accessories like printable worksheets and extra content

- Instructional videos and audio files

- Information about updates, corrections, and new editions

Not every title has accessories, but we're adding new material all the time.

Access free accessories in 3 easy steps:

1. Sign in at NewHarbinger.com (or **register** to create an account).

2. Click on **register a book**. Search for your title and click the **register** button when it appears.

3. Click on the **book cover or title** to go to its details page. Click on **accessories** to view and access files.

That's all there is to it!

If you need help, visit:

NewHarbinger.com/accessories

new harbinger
CELEBRATING
40 YEARS